MONOPOLISTIC COMPETITION AND EFFECTIVE DEMAND

T0319426

MONOPOLISTIC COMPETITION
AND
EFFECTIVE DEMAND

HUKUKANE NIKAIDO

Princeton University Press

Princeton, New Jersey

1975

Library of Congress Cataloging in Publication data will
be found on the last printed page of this book

This book has been composed in Journal Roman

Printed in the United States of America
by Princeton University Press,
Princeton, New Jersey

Preface

Traditional price theory, while it succeeds in elucidating the income distribution aspects of the working of a national economy in the perfectly competitive situation, has lost the economy-wide perspective and has degenerated to the study of market structures and industrial organizations ever since it started exploring the realm of monopoly, oligopoly, and monopolistic competition. Thus, little knowledge is available in the economic literature as to the overall picture of the working of a noncompetitive national economy in spite of the affluence of work in the traditional spirits of oligopoly theory and industrial organizations approach.

This work primarily attempts to fill this gap by presenting a point of departure toward a general equilibrium theoretic study of noncompetitive economies from a *notional* point of view. Just as in the context in which perfect competition and its resulting competitive equilibrium are conceived as notional constructions, rather than a depiction of the real economic world, it aims at conceiving noncompetitive equilibrium states in the economy-wide perspective. It is not meant to be a study of entrepreneurial behaviors within the traditional framework of oligopoly theory.

The work presented in this book has evolved from my research carried out in invaluably favorable and stimulating environments both at University of Minnesota, 1971–1972 and at University of California, Berkeley, in the Fall and Winter Quarters, 1972–1973, under a financial support from Ford Foundation, as a Faculty Research Fellowship and a Rotating Research Professorship, to which many thanks are due. However, the conclusions, opinions, and other statements in this work are mine and are not necessarily those of the foundation.

The earlier version of the results of the research was circulated as "Monopolistic Competition, Objective Demand Functions and the Marxian Labor Value in the Leontief System," Discussion Paper No. 15, May 1972, Center for Economic Research, Department of Economics, University of Minnesota, and "Monopolistic Competition, Objective Demand Functions and the Marxian Labor Value in the Leontief System, II," Working Paper in Economics No. 31, January 1973, Department of Economics, University of California at Berkeley.

I wish to express my indebtedness with sincere gratitude to the following individuals for encouragement, criticism, and suggestions: K. J. Arrow, H. Atsumi, J. S. Chipman, R. Cornwall, G. Debreu, D. Gale, L. Hurwicz, K. Iwai, H. W. Kuhn, D. McFadden, L. W. McKenzie, T. Negishi, R. Radner, M. Richter, P. A. Samuelson, J. Silvestre and K. Suzumura, most of whom were my colleagues during my visit to Minnesota and Berkeley. Needless to say, any remaining error is my responsibility. Acknowledgment is also due to the Institute of Economic Research, Kyoto University, for the technical assistance in the preparation of a final version of the manuscript.

H. N.

Contents

CONTENTS
Chapter V. Welfare Aspects of the Price Mechanism

Chapter VI.   Objective Demand Functions in the Presence
of Capacity Limits

Chapter VII.   Monopolistically Competitive Pricing Modes and
the Objective Demand Functions, Continued

Chapter VIII.   Welfare Aspects of the Price Mechanism, Continued

MONOPOLISTIC COMPETITION AND EFFECTIVE DEMAND

CHAPTER I

Monopolistic Competition and General Equilibrium

I.1 Introduction

The theories of monopolistic or imperfect competition have been well evolved and elaborated through the works of J. Robinson [20], E. H. Chamberlin [3], H. von Stackelberg [21], and others ever since that of A. Cournot [5]. Their works analyze not only the monopolistic or monopolistically competitive behavior of a single firm but also the equilibrium situation of a monopolistically competitive market involving several firms.

Nonetheless, illuminating though the achievements of these authors are, we remain dissatisfied with the present status of our knowledge about monopolistic competition. For even though market equilibria are analyzed, the analyses are worked out from so fatally the partial equilibrium theoretic points of view that they pay little attention to the national economy-wide interdependence of firms. The traditional theories of monopolistic competition always conceal part of the national economy as a closed system of interdependent vital factors, which is hidden and left intact behind the magnificent performances of competing firms in the foreground. Thus, we are dissatisfied with the traditional theories, especially when we are concerned with the income distribution aspects of a noncompetitive national economy, since the lack of attention to the entire economy-wide interdependence prevents them from shedding light on income distribution under monopolistic competition.

It is frequently pointed out that an economy involving monopolistic factors fails to achieve the efficiency of resource allocation. Knowledge of this kind is, however, not far beyond common sense, unless it is based on an analysis of the overall working of the entire economy in question.

R. Triffin [22] rightly emphasizes the need of a general equilibrium theoretic approach to monopolistic competition to pay attention to the interdependent relations among firms. Nonetheless, his image of a well-formulated model of a monopolistically competitive entire national economy is not quite clear. At any rate, everyone is aware that a general equilibrium theoretic viewpoint is undoubtedly needed in order to get insight into the noncompetitive working of the economy peculiar to the present day, and that much work should be done to build general equilibrium theories of non-competitive economies. An attempt to carry out such work seems to involve tremendous difficulty since there is nothing available in the literature on which to base a new clear-cut formulation of a noncompetitive entire national economy, unlike a work based on the well-posed Walrasian general equilibrium formulation of a competitive national economy.

The pioneering work along the lines emphasized above was done by T. Negishi ([15]; [16], Ch. 7) in the early 1960s. This illuminating work is based on the incorporation of monopolists' perceived demand functions into a general equilibrium situation in an ingenious fashion. His result generalizes the Walrasian competitive equilibrium so as to include both perfect competition and monopolistic competition, because perfect competition emerges when the perceived demand functions are of a special form. The crucial line of Negishi's thought, to formulate a monopolistically competitive equilibrium situation, was further elaborated by K. J. Arrow [1] and Arrow and F. H. Hahn ([2], Ch. 6, pp. 151–168). These results, along with Negishi's thought, are the only works available so far in the literature of general equilibrium theories of monopolistic competition. True, they undoubtedly shed much light on the working of the economy under monopolistic competition. But perceived demand functions embody only firms' subjective perception

4

of the economic situation and conjectures as to rival firms' behaviors rather than a direct recognition of the interdependence of firms in the objective sense. A monopolist controls prices or output through the interdependent relations among economic agents in the objective sense even if his decision making is based on a profit estimate in terms of his perceived demand function. So we are still not completely satisfied with our knowledge about monopolistic competition in the general equilibrium context.

The purpose of this work is to illuminate the interdependence of agents in the general equilibrium context in the objective sense by constructing objective demand functions. Much difficulty is inherent in such an attempt. In order to overcome it, this attempt will be pursued in the simple world of the standard Leontief system in which special advantage can be taken of both the well-behavedness of the basic model and the Marxian labor and surplus value concepts. The remaining part of this section will clarify in further detail the unsatisfactory status of theories of monopolistic competition in the general equilibrium context on one hand, and the basic ideas, concepts, methods, and results in this alternative approach on the other, in Sections I.2–I.6.

I.2 Interdependence in the objective sense

In the Walrasian general equilibrium theory, crucial economic magnitudes are mutually interdependent, even when the situation lacks such factors as external economies and diseconomies and consumption externalities making economic agents directly interdependent not just through market mechanism. Interdependence through market mechanism is imposed on every economic agent by the structural characteristics of the economy regardless of whether or not he recognizes it. In general the agent's perception of this interdependence is more or less imperfect and limited. For example, an atomistic consumer in the Walrasian general equilibrium situation is aware only of the current prices, his taste, endowment, and income, but not of the current situation of the market. Nonetheless, interdependent relationships among economic agents, including him, exist and are clear to the omniscient and are embodied in the aggregate market demand and supply or excess demand functions. True, his taste is subjective and peculiar to him, but the aggregate market excess demand functions, which integrate the individual behaviors of all economic agents including his, are given to the market in the objective sense. Interdependence of this kind, which may be referred to as interdependence in the objective sense, must exist even in the general equilibrium situation involving monopolistic competition prior to its more or less imperfect perception by economic agents.

This interdependence in the objective sense in a monopolistically competitive general equilibrium situation is what I intend to establish as one of the purposes in this work. One of the reasons why it is important to establish or realize this interdependence is as follows. An atomistic firm can have an illusion that it is powerful enough to influence the market price formation, even though its influence is practically negligible in the objective sense. A firm whose perceived demand function is steeply downward sloping cannot be a powerful monopolist unless it is practically influential and capable of forcing the market price formation to function through the interdependence in the objective sense toward the goal it desires to achieve. A mere Don Quixote need not be a powerful monopolist.

It should also be noted that a firm's behavioral pattern and the interdependence to which the firm is subjected are different things in principle though they may be intertwined in actuality. The behavioral pattern influences the market price formation, but, conversely, the degree of its influence hinges on, and can be assessed only in terms of, the objective framework of interdependence.

I.3 Subjective versus objective demand functions

In the theories of monopolistic competition, one talks often and easily about the "demand function" of a firm. One is happy enough not to know what it is so long as one's concern is only with the behavior of the firm, or with the monopolistic competition among several firms having respective demand functions. But happiness fades when one becomes seriously interested in the working of a national economy involving monopolistic competition where all economic agents are mutually interdependent in a completely circular way.

Demand for goods must be effective demand coming from the incomes earned by agents in the national economy. The traditional oligopoly theorist pays little attention to the source of effective demand. He lets a monopolist firm seek a maximum of its profit calculated in terms of its demand function. Suppose the maximum monopoly profit is distributed among certain agents. The distributed profit will be spent and will result in the effective demand for goods. Thus, the demand function may have profit as one of its arguments. How ignorant can the theorist be of the possible inconsistency of profit as one of the arguments in the demand function with that as the firm's maximand calculated in terms of the function?

There might be an objection to the above discussion with a possibility in mind that the firm's profit in question is not among the arguments of its demand function. Now, suppose that there are n goods in the economy and that the supply of each good is monopolized by a firm whose demand function may include profits of the firms as its arguments, except its own profit. The oligopoly theorist can hardly ignore such inconsistency even in this special situation. For if the national economy as a closed system of mutually interdependent magnitudes is taken into consideration, the profit of each firm must eventually enter the demand functions of some other firms, though possibly not its own demand function, as arguments, so that the inconsistency problem cannot be ignored in the economy as a whole.

One might regard a firm's demand function as a partly revealed portion of an objective demand function. But this view is not decisive unless the objective demand function as such is unambiguously formulated. It is now a dominant view of general-equilibrium-inclined authors that the demand function of a firm is a perceived or subjective one rather than an objective one. The firm perceives to what extent it is powerful enough to affect the market price formation. The perception may more or less involve the firm's production capacity and the market situation with which the firm is confronted, including its conjectures as to the rival firms' behaviors. The result of the perception is represented in terms of a demand schedule for its product, which is a familiar traditional concept in competitive situations.

As was remarked above, Negishi ([15]; [16], Ch. 7) formulated a general equilibrium situation involving monopolists who seek a maximum profit on the basis of their perceived demand functions, and he proved the existence of an equilibrium. There are loose connections between their perceived demand functions and the actual market situation. The monopolists' profit maximization is shown in his paper to become consistent with the actual market situation at equilibrium, so that the inconsistency problem touched on above is taken care of.

This result of Negishi is the first important pioneering work in the general equilibrium theoretic analysis of monopolistic competition. Nevertheless, it is not completely satisfactory for the following reason, even though it is taken for granted that he is concerned only with solutions of the Cournot-Nash equilibrium point type.

O. Lange ([12], Ch. VII, p. 35)[1] states:

---

[1] Quoted by permission of the publisher.

> The nature of economic equilibrium, as well as of dis-equilibrium, in a monopolistic or monopsonistic market differs from that in a perfectly competitive market. In the latter, disequilibrium consists in excess demand or excess supply. Monopolistic supply, however, is always equal to the demand for the good in question and monopsonistic demand is always equal to supply. A monopolistic or monopsonistic market is in equilibrium when the quantity sold and bought is such that it maximizes the profit of the monopolist or monopsonist.

It is not quite clear here whether Lange was clearly conscious of the distinction between perceived demand functions and objective demand functions. But his lucid characterization of a monopolistic and monopsonistic market in the passages would not be utterly enlightening if objective demand or supply functions were not in his mind.

This characterization, when carried over to the general equilibrium situation, suggests that a monopolistically competitive national economy can be so characterized that demand and supply are balanced for every good in any price situation, while the economy is in equilibrium if, and only if, monopolists' maximizations of their profits are realized consistently and simultaneously. The situation considered by Negishi diverges from that characterized above because "disequilibrium consists in excess demand or excess supply" generally, except in equilibrium at which excess demand and excess supply disappear while the profits of the monopolists are maximized consistently and simultaneously. This comment may apply more aptly to the special case of Negishi's result, where the supply of each good is monopolized by a distinct monopolist who dominates the market of the good in Negishi's terminology, but there are no competitive producers in the economy. It is not clear whether the economy is in a process of tâtonnement when "disequilibrium consists in excess demand or excess supply." Nor is it clear how convincingly monopolists can perceive the demand schedules for their products based on the information data of the markets in which "disequilibrium consists in excess demand or excess supply" generally. All these doubtful points arise from the lack of objective demand functions in Negishi's results.

He also considers a dynamic process of market price formation in which the price of a good whose supply is dominated by a monopolist changes in the direction of the discrepancy between his expected price and the current price. If the market accords with the Lange's characterization of a monopolistic market, the current prices must always equate the demand and supply of the goods in the objective sense. At any rate, this dynamic process does not make much sense unless it is formulated in terms of well-defined objective demand functions.

Negishi's results may, therefore, be thought of as a generalization of competitive equilibrium rather than as an analysis of monopolists' control of the market price formation directly through the national economy-wide framework of interdependence in the objective sense. His results can and will be reconsidered and better reformulated in IV.3 on the basis of objective demand functions, whose construction is one of my purposes in this work.

I.4 Difficulties in the construction of objective demand functions

Now that we have called attention to the importance of interdependence in the objective sense in the analysis of the general equilibrium situation of monopolistic competition, especially, objective demand functions as a specific form of its conceptual representation, it is time to consider difficulties inherent in conceiving and, preferably, constructing them.

First, it should be noted and borne in mind that the very

familiar concept of demand function as such more or less presupposes the presence of competitive atomistic agents who behave as price takers. If no competitive atomistic price taker is involved in the national economy as a closed system, so that it is composed solely of nonatomistic price setters, no demand function can be conceivable. In such a situation, the economy will be a battlefield of bare bargaining, negotiating, and bluffing among all agents, and could be studied only from a purely game theoretic point of view, but not from the traditional point of economic thought based on the concept of demand and supply functions.

A demand function is the representation of integrated behaviors of competitive atomistic agents taking as parameters beyond their control the prices that are the arguments of the function. In this work, I will not be so drastically radical as to eliminate completely any form of demand functions. What I have in mind is a situation in which several competing monopolists are confronted with their respective demand functions for their products. Then, what does distinguish my intention from the traditional lines of thought in the theories of monopolistic competition? There are the integrated behaviors of competitive atomistic agents behind the demand functions of the monopolists as in the traditional theories. But unlike the traditional theories, I am seriously concerned with inquiring into the sources of the demands for their products as effective demand, namely, national income. It is extremely important to realize that the very profits of the monopolists compose directly, or indirectly through their distribution among shareholders, part of the national income in question, while the profits are calculated in terms of the demands and the costs—the latter, too, being in turn a source of the effective demand. There is a circular relation which cannot be ignored in the national economy as a closed system, as was noted in I.3.

When one intends to conceive objective demand functions

as I do, he must take this circular relation into fullest account. His objective demand functions must be constructed in such a way that they are always compatible with the circular relation at any possible price situation. A general equilibrium model of monopolistic competition, which accords with Lange's characterization, can be constructed only when objective demand functions compatible with the circular relation are defined in a clear-cut way. In general this is a difficult task. I will therefore try to pursue this task, as the first step toward a final goal, in the Leontief system, which is simple enough in structure to make the pursuit of the task easier. The pursuit of the task in the Leontief system may also have some bearing on the study of the real economic world from the empirical point of view, unlike a pursuit of the task in a more abstract model.

Mathematically, the construction of well-defined objective demand functions compatible with the circular relation amounts, in this work, to the existence and uniqueness of solutions of certain systems of equations. The existence of solutions will be proved by making use of Brouwer's fixed point theorem, whereas their uniqueness will be ensured by virtue of my previous joint results with D. Gale [9]. Economically, the construction of these functions amounts, in this work, to such a unique determination of sectoral profits at any price situation that the circular relation obtains. These will be done in Chapters III and VI.

Going back to the basic view that a demand function presupposes the presence of competitive atomistic agents and represents their integrated price-taking behaviors, the objective demand functions that will be constructed in Chapter III are based on the assumption that the households of recipients of monopoly profits, too, behave as price takers, their behaviors being included in the functions. Otherwise, the monopoly profits could hardly be represented as the amounts by which the total revenues calculated in terms of well-determinate demand functions exceed the costs, respectively.

I.5 The role of the Marxian labor value

For the contemporary economist the Marxian labor value is something like a will-o'-the-wisp and has been dead and buried. Nevertheless it still has both a metaphysical meaning and a positive, operational meaning in the simple world of the Leontief system, where labor is a unique primary factor of production and capital stock as produced equipments is not binding.

First of all, the labor values of goods, which are defined as the amounts of labor indirectly as well as directly necessary to produce one unit of goods, respectively, are crucial characteristics of the set of all possible final demand vectors, especially its efficient frontier, for a given amount of labor. Then, and therefore, they can serve as natural standard weights to conceive a real aggregate magnitude, a counterpart of the aggregate magnitude in macroeconomic theory. Accordingly it is not utterly groundless for the Marxian economist to talk about the surplus value measured in terms of this magnitude.

The prices of goods diverge more or less from their labor values except in the special situation where there are no profits in any sectors so that both coincide. But, beneath the interplay of the prices on the surface, there is what it essentially means in terms of the labor values. This Marxian-flavored view will prove to be an operationally meaningful one useful in considering the general equilibrium situation of monopolistic competition in the Leontief system, rather than a dogma, as will be made clear in the following sections. In this work, fullest advantage will be taken of this view not in order to foster intentionally the Marxian philosophy, but because the very essential character of the Leontief system logically induces crystal clear representations of certain essential aspects of its working in terms of labor values.

This natural Marxian flavor will be retained as carefully as possible throughout this work. In particular, in presenting

13

the results in the following sections, I will start by reviewing certain known facts about labor values and will then consider surplus value in order to grasp vividly the resource allocative and income distributional implication of pricing for the capitalist class in Chapter II. This approach differs from the orthodox order of presentation, which begins by discussing the construction of objective demand functions.

I.6 Pricing modes in monopolistic competition

In the standard Leontief system of n goods and n sectors, a set of objective demand functions, one for each good, will be constructed in Chapter III. Thus, the ith sector is confronted with the well-determinate demand function for its product, namely, the ith good. The ith sector's demand function is a function of n variables, viz. the prices of the n goods, so that the demand for the ith good depends not only on the price of the good but also on those of the other goods. Moreover, the prices are connected via the inputs coefficients with the labor cost and profit per unit output in such a way that they satisfy the price-determining equations, that is, the equations dual to the output-determining equations in the Leontief system. The demand functions are so constructed that a complete circular relation obtains for the national income comprising total wage bill and total profits at any price situation. Described in a greater detail, the profit of each sector as its maximand always coincides with the profit income earned in this sector as source of part of effective demand at any price situation. The inconsistency that was touched on in the foregoing sections never occurs for the objective demand functions.

Each sector may be composed of a single, several, or many firms. But, for the sake of analytical simplicity, breaking down the sector into individual firms in their possible competition is ignored, so that the sector is thought of as a single decision-making unit. This presumption[2] is not

---

[2] See the appendix at the end of this volume.

unrealistic because, in the real economic world, industries often behave as if they were single decision-making units. The steel industry, auto industry, agriculture, and so forth have unified, strong voices in the battlefield of a nationwide pricing warfare.

It has by now been made clear that the entire national economy, with which I am concerned in this work, is of such a structure that the n sectors (industries) are interdependent in the objective sense through the well-defined objective demand functions. Part, though not all, of the arguments of the functions are at each sector's disposal and capable of being under its control. Each sector is capable of influencing the working of the economy by pricing its product directly or indirectly via the control of the profit per unit output.

This is the bare fundamental aspect of the economy, irrespective of whether or not the sectors are aware of, and perceive, it rightly. Any possible mode of sectoral pricing is effectuated in this framework. If no sector is deceived by its wrong perception of the situation, each sector's maximand will be the sectoral profit calculated in terms of the objective demand function. Thus, a vast field emerges where a great many solution concepts in the theories of games, cooperative or noncooperative, as well as in the traditional theories of monopolistic competition may find applications. More specifically, two special pricing modes are conceivable, namely, joint profit maximization and joint surplus value maximization, which need not be equivalent, as will be shown. On the other hand, if each sector has a perception of the situation that differs from reality, the maximand of each sector will depend on the perception. This alternative situation, too, may admit applications of the solution concepts. In this alternative situation, a solution is feasible only when the perception becomes compatible with the actual state of things represented by the objective demand functions. In other words, the economy is in equilibrium in Lange's sense when and only when the corresponding price situation is a solution at the same time. A typical example is the Negishi solution in the modified form where each sector's actual profit is a maximum of its expected profit calculated in terms of a perceived demand function at the same time.

Thus, a solution concept will single out a set of points, possibly a single point, on the objective demand schedules as an equilibrium state of the economy. This is the basic idea of the present work. Several, though not all, modes of pricing based on alternative solution concepts will be considered in Chapters IV and VII.

CHAPTER II

Surplus Value in the Leontief System

II.1 The Leontief System

In the standard Leontief system of n goods and n sectors let

$A = (a_{ij}) =$ the input coefficients matrix, square of the nth order and nonnegative, which will be assumed to be indecomposable whenever necessary;

$c = (c_i) =$ the final demand vector, n-dimensional and nonnegative;

$v = (v_j) =$ the value added per unit output vector, n-dimensional and nonnegative;

$x = (x_j) =$ the output vector, n-dimensional and nonnegative;

$p = (p_i) =$ the price vector, n-dimensional and nonnegative.

Throughout in this work, the Leontief system is assumed to be viable enough to produce a positive final demand vector, so that the Hawkins-Simon conditions[3] [10] are satisfied. Thus, all the principal minors of the matrix $I - A$, where I is the identity matrix, are positive. Consequently, $I - A$ is nonsingular and its inverse matrix $(I - A)^{-1}$ is nonnegative. Moreover, the output-determining equation

$$(I - A) x = c \tag{II.1}$$

is uniquely solvable in the nonnegative unknown output vector x for any given nonnegative final demand vector c. On the dual side of the system the price-determining equation

$$p'(I - A) = v' \tag{II.2}$$

[3]See also Nikaido ([18], Theorem 6.1, p. 90; [19], Theorem 3.1, p. 14).

17

is uniquely solvable in the nonnegative unknown price vector p for any given nonnegative value added per unit output vector v. These rudimentary and too familiar facts should always be borne in mind.

Now, further let

> $l = (l_j) =$ the labor input vector, n-dimensional and positive;
>
> $\pi = (\pi_j) =$ the profit per unit output vector, n-dimensional and nonnegative, π_j being the jth sector's profit per unit of output;
>
> $w =$ the rate of wage, scalar and positive.

Then, the price-determining equation (II.2) can be rearranged to

$$p'(I - A) = wl' + \pi' \tag{II.3}$$

by breaking down the value added term to wage and profit.

II.2 The capitalists' final demand possibility set and surplus value

The labor values of goods are by definition the total amounts of labor input directly and indirectly necessary to produce units of them. The values cannot be defined separately, but can only be defined simultaneously because of the basic interindustrial relationships in the Leontief system. Specifically, they are defined as a unique solution of Equation (II.3) for $w = 1$, $\pi = 0$. If the solution is denoted by $\sigma = (\sigma_j)$, it is therefore determined by

$$\sigma'(I - A) = l' \tag{II.4}$$

and given by the formula[4]

$$\sigma' = l'(I - A)^{-1}.$$

[4]See Dorfman, Samuelson, and Solow ([6] , Ch. 10, 10.2).

σ is a positive vector by virtue of the indispensability of labor, $l > 0,$[5] and will play a crucial role in the sequel. For the sake of brevity, $\sigma = (\sigma_j)$ and σ_j will be referred to as the labor value vector and the labor value of the jth good, respectively.

The solution p of Equation (II.3) can therefore be represented as

$$p' = w\sigma' + \pi'(I - A)^{-1}. \tag{II.5}$$

Now it is assumed that a labor force consists of many atomistic workers who behave as price takers in supplying labor and demanding goods. Moreover, their behavior is assumed to be represented by an aggregate supply function of labor

$$L(p, w) \tag{II.6}$$

and an aggregate demand function for goods

$$F(p, w) = (F_j(p, w)). \tag{II.7}$$

The following assumptions are imposed on these functions:

[A.1] $L(p, w)$ is a nonnegative, continuous, scalar-valued function of the positive price vector p and the positive rate of wage w.

[A.2] $F(p, w)$ is a nonnegative, continuous, vector-valued function of the positive price vector p and the positive rate of wage w, its jth component being the demand for the jth good.

[A.3] There are no savings from the wage income, which is entirely spent for the purchase of goods. That is, the following identity holds

$$p'F(p, w) = wL(p, w). \tag{II.8}$$

[5] For two n-dimensional vectors $x = (x_i)$ and $y = (y_i)$, $x \geq y$ means $x_i \geq y_i$, $(i = 1, 2, \ldots, n)$, $x \geqq y$ means $x \geq y$ but $x \neq y$, and $x > y$ means $x_i > y_i$, $(i = 1, 2, \ldots, n)$.

[A.4] For any fixed w, the labor supply eventually diminishes to zero, when the prices p_i of all the goods tend to infinity simultaneously. That is,

$$\lim L(p, w) = 0 \quad \text{as} \quad p_i \longrightarrow +\infty \quad \text{simultaneously}$$
$$(i = 1, 2, \ldots, n). \qquad \text{(II.9)}$$

If there is no money illusion, as is assumed in this work, labor can be taken as a numéraire, so that henceforth

$$w = 1, \qquad \text{(II.10)}$$

and Equations (II.5)–(II.9) will be considered only for the case (II.10). Needless to say, this arrangement has nothing to do with the theory of labor value. In (II.5) for $w = 1$, that is,

$$p' = \sigma' + \pi'(I - A)^{-1}, \qquad \text{(II.11)}$$

the sectoral profits are in general nonnegative and possibly positive, so that the prices of goods diverge more or less upward from their labor values.

Finally, an additional assumption is made on a relation between the tastes of workers and the productivity of the underlying technology, namely,

[A.5] The labor force is willing to work at the special price situation $p = \sigma$ and $w = 1$, so that

$$L(\sigma, 1) > 0. \qquad \text{(II.12)}$$

It is now presumed that the economy is of such an institutional structure that each sector is a decision-making unit that carries out production for the benefit of capitalists while being confronted with the atomistic workers characterized above. It is also recalled that the prices of goods are linear functions of the sectoral profits per units of output, as represented in (II.11). With these in mind, let the following sets be defined by

$$C(\pi) = \{c \,|\, c \geq 0, (I - A)\, x = F(p, 1) + c,$$

$$L(p, 1) \geq l'x \text{ for some } x \geq 0\} \qquad \text{(II.13)}$$

$$\Gamma(\pi) = \{c \,|\, c \geq 0, (I - A)\, x = F(p, 1) + c,$$

$$L(p, 1) = l'x \text{ for some } x \geq 0\}. \qquad \text{(II.14)}$$

Given $\pi \geq 0$, then p is determined and so $L(p, 1)$ and $F(p, 1)$. Thus, the sets $C(\pi)$ and $\Gamma(\pi)$ are determinate.

$C(\pi)$ is the set of all possible final demand vectors available to the capitalist class, whereas $\Gamma(\pi)$ is the efficient frontier of $C(\pi)$. As will be made clear, these two sets are always nonempty and of a very simple structure for any given $\pi \geq 0$.

Now, for the sake of economic and mathematical clarity, define

$$M(\pi) = L(p, 1) - o'F(p, 1) \qquad \text{(II.15)}$$

as a function of π. Then, mathematically, the following theorem, which is readily proved, clarifies the crucial properties of $C(\pi)$ and $\Gamma(\pi)$:

Theorem 1. (i) $C(\pi) = \{c \,|\, c \geq 0, M(\pi) \geq o'c\}$, $\Gamma(\pi) = \{c \,|\, c \geq 0, M(\pi) = o'c\}$. (ii) $C(\pi^1) \supset C(\pi^2)$ *if, and only if,* $M(\pi^1) \geq M(\pi^2)$.

Proof. (i) If $c \in C(\pi)$, then from the definitional equation follows

$$x = (I \div A)^{-1} \{F(p, 1) + c\}. \qquad \text{(II.16)}$$

Premultiplying (II.16) by l' one can reduce (II.16) to

$$l'x = o'F(p, 1) + o'c. \qquad \text{(II.17)}$$

(II.17) combined with

$$L(p, 1) \geq l'x, \tag{II.18}$$

gives

$$M(\pi) \geq \sigma'c \tag{II.19}$$

because of (II.15). Conversely, if a nonnegative c satisfies (II.19), then $F(p, 1) + c$ is also nonnegative, so that the x defined by (II.16) is again nonnegative. (II.16), which is equivalent to the definitional equation of $C(\pi)$, can induce (II.17). Finally, (II.17) and (II.19) imply (II.18) because of (II.15). The proof of the assertion for $\Gamma(\pi)$ is essentially the same.

(ii) The assertion is obviously true in the light of the characterization of $C(\pi)$ in (i). Q.E.D.

Geometrically, $C(\pi)$ and $\Gamma(\pi)$ are of a much simpler structure. $C(\pi)$ is a simplex bounded by the hyperplane $M(\pi) = \sigma'c$ and the n coordinate hyperplanes $c_i = 0$ ($i = 1, 2, \ldots, n$), whereas $\Gamma(\pi)$ is a simplex generated as the intersection of the hyperplane $M(\pi) = \sigma'c$ with the nonnegative orthant $R_+^n = \{c \mid c \geq 0\}$. $C(\pi)$ is n-dimensional, and $\Gamma(\pi)$ is $(n - 1)$-dimensional and a face of $C(\pi)$ when $M(\pi) > 0$. $C(\pi) = \Gamma(\pi) = \{0\}$ when $M(\pi) = 0$. Therefore, they are always nonempty (see Figures 1, 2, and 3), as $M(\pi) \geq 0$ for $\pi \geq 0$ from (II.23) below.

Suppose that a profit per unit output vector π is given or possibly chosen by the capitalist class. Then, there will be a supply of $L(p, 1)$ units of labor service, the employment of which leaves any final demand vector c in $C(\pi)$, especially in $\Gamma(\pi)$, at the disposal of the capitalist class after $F_j(p, 1)$ units of the jth good ($j = 1, 2, \ldots, n$) are paid out to the labor force as wages. If the capitalist class is so disposed that the enlargement of the possibility set $C(\pi)$ is a vital problem, as may be likely to be the case, the greater $M(\pi)$, the better.

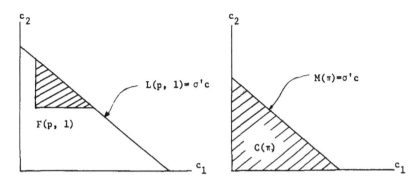

Figure 1   Figure 2

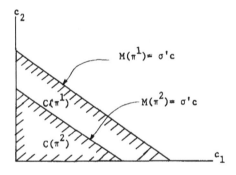

Figure 3

Now, if everything is measured in terms of labor value,

$L(p, 1)$ = net national product
$\sigma'F(p, 1)$ = the wage bill
$M(\pi)$ = surplus value (Mehrwert).

Moreover, in the Marxian scheme of reproduction, the follow-ing equation

$$\sigma'x = \sigma'Ax + \sigma'F(p, 1) + M(\pi)$$

23

where

$$x = (I - A)^{-1} \{F(p, 1) + c\}$$

admits the interpretation

$$\sigma'x = \text{gross national product}$$
$$\sigma'Ax = \text{constant capital}$$
$$\sigma'F(p, 1) = \text{variable capital}$$
$$M(\pi) = \text{surplus value.}$$

From what has been established above, it is now crystal clear that making surplus value $M(\pi)$, a scalar, larger is completely equivalent to the enlargement of $C(\pi)$, the generally n-dimensional final demand possibility set of the capitalist class. In the simple world of the Leontief system this is a fundamental fact that results from the operational function of the labor values of goods in measuring them in real terms beyond any ideological views.

II.3 Maximization of surplus value

In this economy, everything emerges in terms of prices on the surface. Nevertheless, it is essentially of such a structure that its working is effectuated by the capitalist's direct or indirect control of the sectoral profits per unit output π_j, bringing about thereby the allocation of labor in the amount $L(p, 1)$ and the distribution of the net national product $L(p, 1)$ in terms of labor value to the labor force and the capitalist class in the amounts $\sigma'F(p, 1)$ and $M(\pi)$, respectively (by commodity breakdown, $F(p, 1)$ and a final demand vector c from among $C(\pi)$).

This by no means asserts that there is a unique mode of the capitalist's control of π_j. On the contrary, capitalists themselves are likely to be deceived by price phenomena on the surface, so that alternative modes of controlling π_j may be conceivable according to the market structure as well as the capitalist's perception of what is going on beneath the surface. It will be the purpose of Chapter IV to consider these alternative modes after the construction of objective demand functions has been completed in Chapter III.

Here, a special conceivable mode of the capitalist's control of π_j, namely, joint maximization of surplus value will be considered as a polar case. This mode has a normative implication from the capitalist's ethical point of view. For a maximum surplus value, if it ever exists, provides them with the largest possibility set $C(\pi)$ of final demand vectors. If an allotment out from a final demand vector c in a $C(\pi)$ is made to capitalist households that are so disposed that more goods induce greater satisfaction, the allotment can achieve an optimum *among their households* only when π maximizes surplus value. The following theorem ensures the existence of a maximum surplus value.

Theorem 2. *The surplus value $M(\pi)$ is maximized at a π over all $\pi \geq 0$, if the indecomposability of the input coefficients matrix A is explicitly assumed. The corresponding maximum surplus value is positive.*

Proof. By virtue of the indecomposability of A, the inverse of $I - A$ is a positive matrix,[6] as is well known. Hence, all the components of p in Equation (II.11) tend to infinity simultaneously, when even a single component of π tends to infinity, irrespective of whatever behaviors the other components may have. Therefore, by (II.9),

$$\lim_{\pi_j \to +\infty} L(\sigma + (I - A')^{-1}\pi, 1) = 0 \text{ (for each } j). \qquad \text{(II.20)}$$

Define now the set

$$D(\epsilon) = \{\pi \,|\, \pi \geq 0, L(\sigma + (I - A')^{-1}\pi, 1) \geq \epsilon\}. \qquad \text{(II.21)}$$

---

[6]For example, see Nikaido ([18], Theorem 7.4, p. 107; [19], Theorem 20.2, p. 137).

Then, the set is bounded for any positive number $\epsilon > 0$. For otherwise it would include such a sequence $\{\pi^\nu\}$ that

$$\lim_{\nu \to +\infty} \pi_{j\nu} = +\infty \text{ (for some } j). \tag{II.22}$$

But (II.22) contradicts the inclusion of $\{\pi^\nu\}$ in $D(\epsilon)$ because of (II.20).

Now, in the light of (II.8) for $w = 1$ and the definition (II.15), the surplus value can be expressed as

$$M(\pi) = (p - \sigma)'F(p, 1). \tag{II.23}$$

Then, recalling (II.12) in [A.5], one is sure of the positivity of $L(p, 1)$ for a small positive π by continuity. This implies the positivity of some component of $F(p, 1)$ again by (II.8) for $w = 1$, and therefore the positivity of $M(\pi)$ in (II.23) for a small positive π, because $p > \sigma$, $F(p, 1) \geq 0$ then.

Next take such a π that $M(\pi)$ is positive, say, π^0, and let

$$\epsilon = M(\pi^0). \tag{II.24}$$

Then, the set $D(\epsilon)$ contains π^0 and is therefore nonempty, since $L(\sigma + (I - A')^{-1}\pi^0, 1) \geq M(\pi^0)$. On the other hand, if $\pi \notin D(\epsilon)$, then

$$M(\pi) \leq L(\sigma + (I - A')^{-1}\pi, 1) < \epsilon = M(\pi^0).$$

Whence, a maximum of $M(\pi)$ over all nonnegative π's occurs only in $D(\epsilon)$, if any. Likewise a maximum of $M(\pi)$ on $D(\epsilon)$ is its maximum over all nonnegative π's. As was shown, $D(\epsilon)$ is bounded. Moreover, $D(\epsilon)$ is a closed set by virtue of the continuity of $L(\sigma + (I - A')^{-1}\pi, 1)$ in π. Hence $D(\epsilon)$ is a compact set on which the continuous function $M(\pi)$ takes on a maximum, which is not less than ϵ, a positive number.

Q.E.D.

Let π be a solution of this maximization problem. Then, π must satisfy the Kuhn-Tucker condition, if the differentiability of the relevant functions is further assumed, and one has

$$\frac{\partial M(\pi)}{\partial \pi_k} = \sum_{i=1}^{n} b_{ki} \left\{ F_i(p, 1) + \sum_{j=1}^{n} (p_j - \sigma_j) \frac{\partial F_j}{\partial p_i} \right\} \leq 0$$

$$(k = 1, 2, \ldots, n) \qquad (\text{II}.25)$$

with equality holding if $\pi_k > 0$, where

b_{ki} = the (k, i) element of $(I - A)^{-1}$

$$p_j = \sigma_j + \sum_{k=1}^{n} b_{kj} \pi_k \quad (j = 1, 2, \ldots, n)$$

$$\pi_k \geq 0 \qquad\qquad (k = 1, 2, \ldots, n).$$

II.4 The full employment presumption

In the foregoing sections it is presumed that $L(p, 1)$, which is supplied at the current price-wage situation, is fully employed. Even if the capitalist class picks up from among $C(\pi)$ a final demand vector c which is off the efficient frontier $\Gamma(\pi)$, so that less labor than $L(p, 1)$ is virtually needed, $F_j(p, 1)$ units of goods ($j = 1, 2, \ldots, n$) are fully paid out as wages to labor force. Thus, one might imagine if there is any room for the capitalist class to have a larger final demand possibility set than $C(\pi)$ by carrying out production with less employment of labor and the corresponding less wages than those in the full employment level. This section is a digression to see that this does not occur.

To this end, suppose that if μ percent of the labor supply $L(p, 1)$ is employed, the wages paid out are μ percent of the full employment wages $F_j(p, 1)$ ($j = 1, 2, \ldots, n$). Under this generalized mode of employment, the possibility set $C^*(\pi)$ of all final demand vectors available to the capitalist class is the set of all $c \geq 0$ satisfying

$$x = Ax + \{l'x/L(p, 1)\} F(p, 1) + c \qquad (\text{II}.26)$$

$$L(p, 1) \geq l'x \tag{II.27}$$

for some $x \geq 0$

if

$$L(p, 1) > 0.$$

Otherwise $C^*(\pi) = \{0\}$.

(II.26) can easily be rearranged to

$$\left\{ I - \left(A + \frac{F(p, 1)}{L(p, 1)} l' \right) \right\} x = c. \tag{II.28}$$

(II.26) and (II.27) coincide with the definitional equation of $\Gamma(\pi)$ when equality holds in (II.27). Whence $C^*(\pi)$ includes $\Gamma(\pi)$. In the light of (i) in Theorem 1, $\Gamma(\pi)$ contains positive vectors when $M(\pi) > 0$, and hence, so does $C^*(\pi)$. This implies that the left-hand side of (II.28) is a positive vector for some $x \geq 0$. Since the matrix

$$A + \frac{F(p, 1)}{L(p, 1)} l'$$

is nonnegative, it follows from what has been shown above that the coefficients matrix of (II.28) is nonsingular and has its inverse nonnegative.[7] Therefore, when $M(\pi) > 0$, $C^*(\pi)$ is nothing but the set of all nonnegative c satisfying

$$L(p, 1) \geq l' \left\{ I - \left(A + \frac{F(p, 1)}{L(p, 1)} l' \right) \right\}^{-1} c. \tag{II.29}$$

It is now obvious by the positivity of

$$l' \left\{ I - \left(A + \frac{F(p, 1)}{L(p, 1)} l' \right) \right\}^{-1}$$

---

[7]For example, see Nikaido ([18], Theorem 6.3, p. 95; [19], Theorem 3.1, p. 14, and Theorem 15.3, p. 113).

that the efficient frontier of $C^*(\pi)$ is composed of all non-negative c satisfying (II.29) with equality and coincides with $\Gamma(\pi)$. This proves $C^*(\pi) = C(\pi)$.

It remains to consider the case $M(\pi) = 0$, which implies that

$$C(\pi) = \{0\} \tag{II.30}$$

by (i) in Theorem 1, and that

$$L(p, 1) = \sigma'F(p, 1) \tag{II.31}$$

by (II.15). Then, premultiplying the coefficients matrix of (II.28) by $\sigma' = l'(I - A)^{-1}$, one gets, in view of (II.31),

$$\sigma'\left\{I - \left(A + \frac{F(p, 1)}{L(p, 1)}l'\right)\right\} = 0'.$$

Whence

$$\sigma'c = 0 \tag{II.32}$$

for any nonnegative c expressible by (II.28). Since σ is a positive vector, this entails $c = 0$. Thus, $C^*(\pi) = \{0\}$ and coincides with $C(\pi)$ in (II.30).

The discussion above may justify the full employment presumption in this work. The reserve army of labor force will therefore not explicitly show up here.

CHAPTER III

Objective Demand Functions

III.1 Capitalists' choice of final demand

The foregoing analysis, which is worked out in terms of the labor and surplus values in Chapter II, by no means intends to give a description of what is going on as economic phenomena in the orthodox sense. It simply describes what is going on in terms of the labor value behind the scenes of economic phenomena. The behaviors of economic agents such as capitalists and workers are very likely to be based on something on the surface of the interplay of prices, rather than on the labor value concept beneath it. Nonetheless, whatever behavioral principles may bring about a final economic equilibrium, the resource allocative significance of the equilibrium can be assessed in terms of the labor value in an operationally meaningful way, free from ideological dogma. For this reason, the presentation of the results is given intentionally in a reverse order, starting at the consideration of what is going on in the realm of the labor value, then proceeding to the analysis of the factual working of the economy, rather than starting at a setup of behavioral principles of economic agents, then discussing the working of the economy brought about by them and finally interpreting it possibly in terms of the labor value. Before proceeding to the main issue in this chapter this peculiar character of the presentation is emphasized again in order to prevent the author's intention in this work from being misunderstood.

It has been made clear in the preceding chapter that if a nonnegative profit per unit output vector π is given, then the price vector is determined by Equation (II.11), and the possibility set of final demand vectors $C(\pi)$ and its efficient frontier $\Gamma(\pi)$ are available to the capitalist class. True, the determination of π is effected in the factual working of the economy through a market mechanism that is either competitive, monopolistically competitive, or of yet another nature. But, whatever pricing principle may determine π, a given π provides the capitalist class with the possibility set $C(\pi)$, from among which the capitalist class can pick up any final demand vector c. As a matter of fact, the production activities of sectors represented by the gross output vector x are influenced, and determined through Equation (II.16), by the choice of c from among $C(\pi)$. Therefore different c's in $C(\pi)$ are supplied by virtue of different gross output vectors. At any rate, the capitalist class can choose any c from among $C(\pi)$ by virtue of the accomplishment of the corresponding production activities.

How then a final demand vector c is chosen by the capitalist class from among $C(\pi)$ naturally hinges on what motivates capitalists as consumers or, more precisely, as demanders of goods for their own use. It is noted that the c is the remainder when the workers' demand $F(p, 1)$ and the derived demand Ax are deducted from the gross output x. The capitalists might negotiate directly about the bill of goods to be produced and the distribution of the product among themselves, not by way of a market mechanism. But in a capitalist economy such as we consider here, both the choice of a final demand vector from among $C(\pi)$ and its distribution are most likely to be worked out through a market mechanism. The capitalists themselves are imprisoned in a market mechanism. They, as producers and entrepreneurs, can possibly influence price formation in the markets to a certain extent, depending on the market structures. But as demanders of goods for their own use, they, too, are subjected to the price system that is more or less controlled by themselves. The profits earned are distributed among the households of capitalists. The households spend their profit income to purchase goods. Notwithstanding the possible control of prices by the capitalists as entrepreneurs, their households are very likely to take the prices as given parameters and to behave as competitive consumers in spending their profit income for the purchase of goods that they demand for their own use.

Now, if the above presumption as to the behaviors of the households of capitalists is taken for granted, there will be effective demand originating from the profit income for the product which is supplied by the choice of a final demand vector c from among $C(\pi)$. The factual choice of a final demand vector and its distribution among the capitalists are thereby worked out when the demand equals the supply. It is the purpose of this chapter to see how these are worked out.

To this end, an aggregate demand function of the capitalists' households for goods will be introduced in parallel with the workers' demand function $F(p, w)$ and on the basis of the above presumption. Let $s_i(i = 1, 2, \ldots, n)$ be the total profit of the ith sector. The aggregate demand function of the capitalists' households

$$G(p, s_1, s_2, \ldots, s_n) = (G_j(p, s_1, s_2, \ldots, s_n)) \qquad \text{(III.1)}$$

is required to satisfy the following assumptions:

[B.1] $G(p, s_1, s_2, \ldots, s_n)$ is a nonnegative, continuous vector-valued function of the positive price vector p and the nonnegative sectoral profits $s_i(i = 1, 2, \ldots, n)$, its jth component being the demand for the jth good.

[B.2] $G(p, s_1, s_2, \ldots, s_n)$ has either of the following two spending patterns:

J. B. Say's case: The profit income is entirely spent for the purchase of goods. That is, the following identity holds

$$p'G(p, s_1, s_2, \ldots, s_n) = \sum_{j=1}^{n} s_j. \qquad \text{(III.2)}$$

Keynesian case: There are savings from the profit income. More specifically, there exists a constant[8] θ fulfilling

$$1 > \theta > 0 \tag{III.3}$$

such that the following inequality holds identically

$$p'G(p, s_1, s_2, \ldots, s_n) \leq \theta \sum_{j=1}^{n} s_j. \tag{III.4}$$

It is noted that, in Say's case, (III.2) need not imply that the spending of the profit income is exclusively for the purchase of consumption goods. The demand function can possibly include demand for goods for investment. However, it is in better accord with the spirit of Keynesian income analysis to assume the Keynesian case above.

Before proceeding to the main discussion, it should be recalled and borne in mind that, although the demand function includes p as an argument, p, which need not be a surplus value maximizing price vector, is assumed to be given and kept constant for a while. Suppose that a final demand vector c is chosen from among $C(\pi)$, in particular, its efficient frontier $\Gamma(\pi)$. As was remarked, the supply of c is effected by the production activities in the corresponding gross output $x(c)$ determined by (II.16). The profit per unit output vector π being already given, the profit of the jth sector is

$$s_j(c) = \pi_j x_j(c) \quad (j = 1, 2, \ldots, n). \tag{III.5}$$

Then, there will be effective demand for goods originating from these profit incomes' (III.5) at the price vector p. However, the effective demand represented by the demand function need not equal the supply c. Does there exist any special c in $C(\pi)$ such that demand equals supply in the above sense? The consistent working of the economy is effectuated by and

---

[8]θ need not be a constant, but can be a function of p in the reasoning below.

only by choosing such a special c from among $C(\pi)$, if any. For convenience the choice of this special final demand vector c equating demand to supply will henceforth be referred to as a competitive choice. The next step is to prove the existence of a competitive choice in both Say's and Keynesian cases.

III.2 Existence of a competitive choice

It is clear from the definition of a competitive choice that there is a complete circulation of national income flow brought about by this choice. All the wages and profits earned induce effective demand that exactly equals the product supplied, while the very equality of demand to supply makes the profit determinate *ex post* in addition to the predetermined wages.

There is a crucial relationship between the circulation of national income flow and the feasibility and efficiency expressed in terms of the labor value of the supply of a final demand vector c. This relationship, which holds true regardless of the introduction of the demand function $G(p, s_1, s_2, \ldots, s_n)$, is of independent interest and of much relevance to the subsequent discussion at the same time. This relationship will be given for easier reference in the sequel in a theorem.

Theorem 3. *For any final demand vector c, which need not belong to $C(\pi)$, and the corresponding gross output vector $x(c)$ determined by (II.16), namely,*

$$x(c) = (I - A)^{-1} \{F(p, 1) + c\} \tag{III.6}$$

the relationship

$$\pi'x(c) = M(\pi) - o'c + p'c \tag{III.7}$$

holds. In particular, the ex ante profit $\pi'x(c)$ equals

34

the monetary value of supply $p'c$,

$$\pi'x(c) = p'c \tag{III.8}$$

if and only if c belongs to the efficient frontier $\Gamma(\pi)$ of $C(\pi)$.

Proof. The proof is easy and immediate. In fact, pre-multiplying (III.6) by π' and taking (II.11) into account, one has

$$\pi'x(c) = (p - \sigma)' \{F(p, 1) + c\}. \tag{III.9}$$

Then, the relationship (III.7) follows from (III.9), if one recalls a representation of the surplus value $M(\pi)$ in (II.23).

Q.E.D.

It is further noted that the relationship (III.7) translates the relation of the *ex ante* profit $\pi'x(c)$ to the monetary value of supply $p'c$ into its resource allocative significance in terms of the labor value. In fact, if c is feasible, $c \in C(\pi)$, but not efficient, $c \notin \Gamma(\pi)$, then the *ex ante* profit income exceeds the monetary value of supply,

$$\pi'x(c) > p'c. \tag{III.10}$$

On the other hand, if c is infeasible, $c \notin C(\pi)$, then the *ex ante* profit income is insufficient to purchase the proposed supply. The equality of the *ex ante* profit income to the *ex ante* supply value obtains if and only if a final demand vector c in the efficient frontier $\Gamma(\pi)$ is supplied. It goes without saying, however, that (III.8) does not necessarily imply equality of demand to supply by commodity breakdown, which can be brought about only by a competitive choice of c, as will be seen below.

Theorem 4. (Existence of a competitive choice in Say's case.) *There exists a final demand vector c in the efficient* *frontier* $\Gamma(\pi)$ *such that (III.6) and*

$$c = G(p, \pi_1 x_1(c), \pi_2 x_2(c), \ldots, \pi_n x_n(c)) \qquad \text{(III.11)}$$

holds.

Proof. If $M(\pi) = 0$, then $\Gamma(\pi)$ contains only one vector, $c = 0$. On the other hand, $\pi'x(0) = 0$ from (III.7) for $c = 0$ and $M(\pi) = 0$. Then, in view of (III.5), one sees that the right-hand side is vanishing in (III.2). Hence

$$p'G(p, \pi_1 x_1(0), \pi_2 x_2(0), \ldots, \pi_n x_n(0)) = 0.$$

But $G(p, s_1, s_2, \ldots, s_n)$ is nonnegative-valued by assumption [B.1], and p is positive, so that the right-hand side of (III.11) is the zero vector for $c = 0$. This proves that (III.11) obtains for the only possible $c = 0$ in $\Gamma(\pi)$ in case $M(\pi) = 0$.

Next, suppose $M(\pi) > 0$. As was noted, $\Gamma(\pi)$ is an $(n - 1)$-dimensional simplex. Define a mapping $\phi : \Gamma(\pi) \longrightarrow \Gamma(\pi)$ by the formula that assigns with any $c \in \Gamma(\pi)$ the image

$$\phi(c) = \frac{M(\pi) \, G(p, \pi_1 x_1(c), \pi_2 x_2(c), \ldots, \pi_n x_n(c))}{\sigma'G(p, \pi_1 x_1(c), \pi_2 x_2(c), \ldots, \pi_n x_n(c))}.$$

$$\text{(III.12)}$$

It will be remarked that the construction of the mapping can be worked out in a consistent way. In fact, it follows from $\sigma'c = M(\pi) > 0$ that the nonnegative c has at least one component positive. Hence, $p'c > 0$ by the positivity of p. Therefore $\pi'x(c) > 0$ by (III.8). One sees, in view of (III.2) and (III.5), that $p'G(p, \pi_1 x_1(c), \pi_2 x_2(c), \ldots, \pi_n x_n(c)) > 0$. This implies that the nonnegative $G(p, \pi_1 x_1(c), \pi_2 x_2(c), \ldots, \pi_n x_n(c))$ has at least one component positive. Thus, the denominator, which is the inner product of the positive vector σ and $G(p, \pi_1 x_1(c), \pi_2 x_2(c), \ldots, \pi_n x_n(c))$, must be positive for any c in $\Gamma(\pi)$. On the other hand, $\phi(c)$ is always nonnegative and $\sigma'\phi(c) = M(\pi)$ by construction. Therefore,

ϕ is a well-defined mapping from $\Gamma(\pi)$ into $\Gamma(\pi)$. Finally, ϕ is continuous because of the continuity of $G(p, \pi_1 x_1(c), \pi_2 x_2(c), \ldots, \pi_n x_n(c))$.

Therefore, by virtue of the well-known Brouwer fixed point theorem, ϕ has a fixed point $\hat{c}$ such that

$$\hat{c} = \frac{M(\pi) \, G(p, \pi_1 x_1(\hat{c}), \pi_2 x_2(\hat{c}), \ldots, \pi_n x_n(\hat{c}))}{\sigma' G(p, \pi_1 x_1(\hat{c}), \pi_2 x_2(\hat{c}), \ldots, \pi_n x_n(\hat{c}))}.$$

(III.13)

Premultiplication of (III.13) by p' gives, in the light of (III.2), (III.5), and (III.8),

$$p'\hat{c} = \frac{M(\pi) \, p'\hat{c}}{\sigma' G(p, \pi_1 x_1(\hat{c}), \pi_2 x_2(\hat{c}), \ldots, \pi_n x_n(\hat{c}))},$$

(III.14)

which implies

$$M(\pi) = \sigma' G(p, \pi_1 x_1(\hat{c}), \pi_2 x_2(\hat{c}), \ldots, \pi_n x_n(\hat{c}))$$

because $p'\hat{c} > 0$. Whence (III.13) reduces to

$$\hat{c} = G(p, \pi_1 x_1(\hat{c}), \pi_2 x_2(\hat{c}), \ldots, \pi_n x_n(\hat{c})),$$

and the choice of this $\hat{c}$ is a competitive choice, as was to be shown.   Q.E.D.

Theorem 5. (Existence of a competitive choice in Keynesian case.) *Let $d \geq 0$ be a given investment composition vector which is constant.*[9] *Then, there exist a final demand vector c and a nonnegative scalar ω such that*

$$\omega d + c \in \Gamma(\pi)$$

(III.15)

$$x = (I - A)^{-1} \{F(p, 1) + \omega d + c\}$$

(III.16)

---

[9]d need not be a constant vector, but can be a vector-valued function of p and the sectoral profits in the argument below.

$$c = G(p, \pi_1 x_1, \pi_2 x_2, \ldots, \pi_n x_n). \tag{III.17}$$

The above ω is positive if and only if $M(\pi) > 0$.

Proof. Before proceeding to the proof, it is noted that the capitalist class picks up $\omega d + c$ from among $C(\pi)$ because of the presence of demand for investment goods ωd, rather than a mere c. However, Theorem 3 is still valid provided the c in the statement of the theorem is replaced by $\omega d + c$.

The proof will be worked out by obtaining a solution as a fixed point of a mapping, which is constructed in a different way. The mapping to be constructed here is defined for all nonnegative vectors c, which need not belong to $C(\pi)$, unlike the mapping in the preceding theorem. First of all, a nonnegative numerical function $\omega(c)$ is defined for all $c \geq 0$ by the formula

$$\omega(c) = \begin{cases} \dfrac{M(\pi) - \sigma'c}{\sigma'd} & \text{if } M(\pi) > \sigma'c \\ 0 & \text{otherwise.} \end{cases} \tag{III.18}$$

The function $\omega(c)$ is continuous on the set of all $c \geq 0$.
    Next let

$$x(c) = (I - A)^{-1} \{F(p, 1) + \omega(c)d + c\}. \tag{III.19}$$

Then with respect to (III.19) one obtains as a counterpart equation to (III.7)

$$\pi'x(c) = M(\pi) - \sigma'(\omega(c)d + c) + p'(\omega(c)d + c). \tag{III.20}$$

Now, denoting the set of all nonnegative vectors c in the n-dimensional Euclidean space R^n, the so-called nonnegative orthant, by R_+^n, define a mapping $\psi : R_+^n \longrightarrow R_+^n$ by the formula

$$\psi(c) = G(p, \pi_1 x_1(c), \pi_2 x_2(c), \ldots, \pi_n x_n(c)). \tag{III.21}$$

It is intended that a solution may be found as a fixed

point of the mapping ψ. But the Brouwer fixed point theorem is not directly applicable to the mapping, since the original domain on which it is defined is the entire R_+^n, an unbounded set. To overcome this difficulty, the mapping will be considered within a suitably chosen bounded subset of the entire domain.

To this end, the following inequality will be established:

$$p'\psi(c) \leq p'c \qquad\qquad\qquad (III.22)$$

for any c satisfying

$$c \geq 0, p'c \geq \frac{\theta p'dM(\pi)}{(1 - \theta)\sigma'd} \qquad\qquad (III.23)$$

where θ is the θ given in the Keynesian case of [B.2]. In fact, in view of (III.21), (III.4) and (III.20), one sees for any $c \geq 0$

$$p'\psi(c) = p'G(p, \pi_1 x_1(c), \pi_2 x_2(c), \ldots, \pi_n x_n(c))$$

$$\leq \theta \, \pi'x(c) \qquad\qquad\qquad (III.24)$$

$$= \theta \, \{M(\pi) - \sigma'(\omega(c)d + c) + p'(\omega(c)d + c)\}.$$

It is obvious from the definition of $\omega(c)$ that

$$M(\pi) \leq \sigma'(\omega(c)d + c) \qquad\qquad (III.25)$$

$$\omega(c) \leq \frac{M(\pi)}{\sigma'd} . \qquad\qquad\qquad (III.26)$$

By taking (III.25) and (III.26) into account, one can reduce (III.24) to

$$p'\psi(c) \leq \frac{\theta p'dM(\pi)}{\sigma'd} + \theta p'c. \qquad\qquad (III.27)$$

The right-hand side of (III.27) is not greater for any c satisfying (III.23) than $p'c$. Whence (III.22) follows.

Now consider the set

$$\Omega = \left\{ c \,\middle|\, c \geq 0, \;\; \frac{\theta p' dM(\pi)}{(1 - \theta)\sigma'd} \geq p'c \right\}. \tag{III.28}$$

Ω is a compact set, since p is a positive vector. Therefore the image $\psi(\Omega)$ of Ω under the mapping ψ is also compact because of the continuity of ψ. Hence $\psi(\Omega)$ is bounded, so that it can be included in a simplex

$$\Delta = \{ c \,|\, c \geq 0, \;\; \delta \geq p'c \}$$

for a sufficiently large positive δ. That is

$$\Delta \supset \psi(\Omega). \tag{III.29}$$

It will be shown that ψ maps each c in Δ into Δ. In fact, let c be a point in Δ. If $c \in \Omega$, then $\psi(c) \in \psi(\Omega) \subset \Delta$ by (III.29). If $c \notin \Omega$, then

$$\frac{\theta p' dM(\pi)}{(1 - \theta)\sigma'd} < p'c,$$

so that (III.22) holds and hence $p'\psi(c) \leq p'c \leq \delta$, implying $\psi(c) \in \Delta$.

Now, confining the domain of ψ to Δ, a compact and convex set, one can apply the Brouwer fixed point theorem to the continuous mapping $\psi : \Delta \longrightarrow \Delta$. Thus, ψ has a fixed point $\hat{c}$,

$$\hat{c} = \psi(\hat{c}). \tag{III.30}$$

It is obvious that this $\hat{c}$ and the corresponding $\omega = \omega(\hat{c})$ satisfy Equations (III.16) and (III.17). It remains to show that they satisfy (III.15). To show this, it suffices to see that $\omega(\hat{c})d + \hat{c}$ is feasible, i.e., $\omega(\hat{c})d + \hat{c} \in C(\pi)$. For, if it is feasible, then $M(\pi) \geq \sigma'(\omega(\hat{c})d + \hat{c})$ by definition, which turns out to be $M(\pi) = \sigma'(\omega(\hat{c})d + \hat{c})$ by (III.25).

With this in mind, suppose that $\omega(\hat{c})d + \hat{c}$ is infeasible, so that strict inequality holds in (III.25). Then,

$$\omega(\hat{c}) = 0, \tag{III.31}$$

and inequality (III.24) for $c = \hat{c}$ reduces under (III.30) and (III.31) to

$$p'\hat{c} \leq \theta p'\hat{c}. \tag{III.32}$$

But (III.32) is impossible, since $1 > \theta > 0$ and $p'\hat{c} > 0$. Here, $p'\hat{c} > 0$ is seen in the following way. In fact, $\sigma'\hat{c} > 0$ is implied by (III.25) in a strict inequality form and (III.31). This shows that the nonnegative $\hat{c}$ has at least one positive component. Hence $p'\hat{c} > 0$ because $p > 0$.

Finally, the supplementary assertion as to the nonvanishingness of ω in a solution will be considered. In fact, if $M(\pi) = 0$, then $\omega d + c = 0$ by feasibility (III.15), since $\Gamma(\pi) = \{0\}$ in this case. This clearly implies $\omega = 0$. Conversely, if $\omega = 0$, then $c \in \Gamma(\pi)$, and hence $M(\pi) = \sigma'c$. Therefore, inequality (III.24) reduces to $p'c \leq \theta p'c$, which implies $p'c = 0$ under $1 > \theta > 0$. Thus $c = 0$ because of the nonnegativity of c and the positivity of p. This proves $M(\pi) = \sigma'c = 0$. It is thereby shown that ω is positive if and only if $M(\pi) > 0$. The proof is now complete.   Q.E.D.

In Theorems 4 and 5, the competitive choices are formulated in terms of certain equations in the unknowns c and ω. But they can be reformulated in terms of equations in the gross output x and the above ω as unknowns.

In fact, the competitive choice in Say's case can be reformulated as the determination of the gross output vector x by virtue of the equation[10]

$$x = (I - A)^{-1} \{F(p, 1) + G(p, \pi_1 x_1, \pi_2 x_2, \ldots, \pi_n x_n)\}. \tag{III.33}$$

---

[10]Equations (III.33) and (III.35) are counterparts of equations studied by D. Gale [8] and the author ([17]; [18], Ch. III, Section 11) in connection with the determination and propagation of multi-sectoral incomes.

On the other hand, the competitive choice in the Keynesian case can be reformulated as the determination of the gross output vector x and the scale of investment ω by virtue of the equations

$$\omega d + G(p, \pi_1 x_1, \pi_2 x_2, \ldots, \pi_n x_n) \in \Gamma(\pi) \qquad \text{(III.34)}$$

$$x = (I - A)^{-1}\{F(p, 1) + \omega d + G(p, \pi_1 x_1, \pi_2 x_2, \ldots, \pi_n x_n)\}.$$
$$\text{(III.35)}$$

Thus, the competitive choice discussed above is actually the determination of national income of a Keynesian type at the fixed price system not only in the Keynesian case but also even in the Say's case.[11] If $\omega > 1$ in the solution, (III.35) would determine a true Keynesian underemployment equilibrium for $\omega = 1$.

III.3 Uniqueness of competitive choice

In general the competitive choice, whose existence has been proved in Theorems 4 and 5, is not necessarily unique. It is therefore of interest and even important to see under what conditions its uniqueness obtains, all the more as uniqueness is required in order to construct single-valued objective demand functions.

There might be possible alternative conditions for uniqueness. Here certain sufficient conditions for uniqueness will be discussed. These conditions, which slightly specify the spending patterns of the capitalist households as embodied in the demand function $G(p, s_1, s_2, \ldots, s_n)$, ensure the uniqueness of competitive choice under differentiability. Under the differentiability assumption, the relevant concepts and discussion pertaining to uniqueness become transparent. Thus the analysis will be worked out in this section as well as elsewhere below under differentiability:

---

[11]Reference to J. B. Say is made because supply creates demand for it in its aggregate value in this case.

[B.3] $G(p, s_1, s_2, \ldots, s_n)$ is differentiable[12] in the rectangular region $s_i \geq 0$ $(i = 1, 2, \ldots, n)$.

The principal additional assumption on the spending patterns of the capitalist households, which ensures the uniqueness of competitive choice, is the hypothesis of the absence of inferior goods.[13] The hypothesis means that the demand function $G(p, s_1, s_2, \ldots, s_n)$ is monotonically non-decreasing with respect to the arguments $s_1, s_2, \ldots, s_n$ for each fixed p. Under differentiability, the hypothesis is expressed as the nonnegativity of the partial derivatives

$$\frac{\partial G_i}{\partial s_j} = G_{ij}(p, s_1, s_2, \ldots, s_n) \geq 0 \quad (i, j = 1, 2, \ldots, n)$$

$$(\text{III.36})$$

The hypothesis of no inferior goods suffices to ensure the uniqueness of competitive choice in the Say's case.

In order to ensure the uniqueness of competitive choice in the Keynesian case, however, the hypothesis must be reinforced by yet another additional assumption on the

---

[12]It is meant by differentiability that each component function $G_i(p, s_1, s_2, \ldots, s_n)$ has a total differential

$$dG_i = \sum_{j=1}^{n} (\partial G_i / \partial s_j) ds_j$$

such that the difference between $G_i(p, s_1 + ds_1, s_2 + ds_2, \ldots, s_n + ds_n)$ and $G_i(p, s_1, s_2, \ldots, s_n) + dG_i$ is an infinitesimal magnitude of order higher than

$$\sqrt{\sum_{j=1}^{n} (ds_j)^2}.$$

See Gale and Nikaido [9] and Nikaido ([18], Ch. I, Section 5.3).

[13]Under the hypothesis of no inferior goods, D. Gale [8] has proved uniqueness in a simple elegant way without differentiability. However, the proof relies on less-than-one marginal propensities to spend and the separability of demand in such a sense that demand is a sum of sectoral demands dependent only on their own sectoral profit income. It seems to be inapplicable to the present cases.

spending patterns, namely, the hypothesis of no-greater-than-one marginal propensities to spend, which means

$$\sum_{i=1}^{n} p_i \frac{\partial G_i}{\partial s_j} \leq 1 \quad (j = 1, 2, \ldots, n). \tag{III.37}$$

(III.37) is prevalent, especially when the average propensity to spend

$$\theta(p, s_1, s_2, \ldots, s_n) = \frac{p'G(p, s_1, s_2, \ldots, s_n)}{\displaystyle\sum_{k=1}^{n} s_k} \tag{III.38}$$

is nonincreasing with respect to the arguments $s_1, s_2, \ldots, s_n$ in the Keynesian case. For upon differentiation of (III.38), one sees

$$\sum_{i=1}^{n} p_i \frac{\partial G_i}{\partial s_j} = \theta(p, s_1, s_2, \ldots, s_n) + \left(\sum_{k=1}^{n} s_k\right) \frac{\partial}{\partial s_j}$$

$$\theta(p, s_1, s_2, \ldots, s_n) < 1 \quad (j = 1, 2, \ldots, n),$$

because of $\theta(p, s_1, s_2, \ldots, s_n) < 1$ implied by (III.3) and (III.4), and the nonincreasing average propensity to spend

$$\frac{\partial}{\partial s_j} \theta(p, s_1, s_2, \ldots, s_n) \leq 0 \quad (j = 1, 2, \ldots, n).$$

Now, the way that uniqueness is ensured in a natural way by the above additional assumptions of economic significance will be seen below. All the basic assumptions such as [B.1], [B.2], and so forth are still to be premised and will be used without explicit references thereto.

Theorem 6. (Uniqueness of competitive choice in Say's case.) *Under differentiability, if there are no inferior goods* *for the capitalist households, then the competitive choice is unique. That is, the solution c of Equation (III.11), with $x(c)$ defined by (III.6), is unique.*

Proof. Let equation (III.11) be rearranged as

$$H_i(c) = c_i - G_i(p, \pi_1 x_1(c), \pi_2 x_2(c), \ldots, \pi_n x_n(c)) = 0$$

$$(i = 1, 2, \ldots, n). \qquad \text{(III.39)}$$

It is recalled that a solution of (III.39) is obtained as a fixed point of a mapping from $\Gamma(\pi)$ into $\Gamma(\pi)$. Moreover, any solution of (III.39) must automatically lie on $\Gamma(\pi)$. It must satisfy $p'c = \pi'x(c)$ by (III.2) and (III.39), so that $c \in \Gamma(\pi)$ by Theorem 3. Nonetheless, Equation (III.39) is to be considered on the entire set of all nonnegative c's, namely, the nonnegative orthant R_+^n, when it comes to the uniqueness of solution.

With this remark in mind, the Jacobian matrix

$$J_H(c) = \left(\frac{\partial H_i}{\partial c_j}\right) \qquad \text{(III.40)}$$

of the mapping $H : R_+^n \longrightarrow R^n$, where $H(c) = (H_i(c))$, will be evaluated. By performing differentiation in view of (III.6), one obtains

$$J_H(c) = I - \left(\frac{\partial G_i}{\partial s_j}\right) \begin{pmatrix} \pi_1 & & & 0 \\ & \pi_2 & & \\ & & \ddots & \\ 0 & & & \pi_n \end{pmatrix} (I - A)^{-1} \qquad \text{(III.41)}$$

where I is the identity matrix of the nth order. The matrix $(\partial G_i/\partial s_j)$, which is a function of c, is a nonnegative matrix by virtue of the hypothesis of no inferior goods. The matrix between $(\partial G_i/\partial s_j)$ and $(I - A)^{-1}$ in (III.41) is a diagonal matrix with π_i's in its principal diagonal. Hence the matrix

$$\left(\frac{\partial G_i}{\partial s_j}\right) \begin{pmatrix} \pi_1 & & & 0 \\ & \pi_2 & & \\ & & \ddots & \\ 0 & & & \pi_n \end{pmatrix} (I - A)^{-1} \qquad \text{(III.42)}$$

is a nonnegative matrix.

Next, differentiating (III.2) with respect to s_j, one sees that

$$\sum_{i=1}^{n} p_i \frac{\partial G_i}{\partial s_j} = 1 \quad (j = 1, 2, \ldots, n), \qquad \text{(III.43)}$$

holds, or in a matrix form

$$p' \left(\frac{\partial G_i}{\partial s_j}\right) = (1, 1, \ldots, 1). \qquad \text{(III.44)}$$

Whence follows

$$p' \left(\frac{\partial G_i}{\partial s_j}\right) \begin{pmatrix} \pi_1 & & & 0 \\ & \pi_2 & & \\ & & \ddots & \\ 0 & & & \pi_n \end{pmatrix} = \pi'. \qquad \text{(III.45)}$$

Therefore, in the light of (III.45) and (II.11), one can evaluate

$$p' J_H (c) = p' - p' \left(\frac{\partial G_i}{\partial s_j}\right) \begin{pmatrix} \pi_1 & & & 0 \\ & \pi_2 & & \\ & & \ddots & \\ 0 & & & \pi_n \end{pmatrix} (I - A)^{-1}$$

$$= p' - \pi' (I - A)^{-1} \qquad \text{(III.46)}$$

$$= p' - (p' - \sigma')$$

$$= \sigma' > 0',$$

which gives an important result

$$\begin{cases} p' J_H (c) = \sigma' > 0' \\ p > 0, \quad \sigma > 0. \end{cases} \qquad \text{(III.47)}$$

Since $J_H(c)$ is the identity matrix minus a nonnegative matrix, (III.47) implies by virtue of the well-known Hawkins-Simon's result [10] that all the principal minors of $J_H(c)$ are positive on the domain of the mapping R_+^n, a rectangular region. Therefore, the solution of Equation (III.39) is unique by virtue of a univalence theorem on a mapping having a P-Jacobian matrix due to D. Gale and myself ([9], Theorem 4; Nikaido [18], Theorem 20.4, p. 370). Q.E.D.

Theorem 7. (Uniqueness of competitive choice in Keynesian case.) *Under differentiability, if there are no inferior goods for the capitalist households, and if their marginal propensities to spend never exceed one, then the competitive choice is unique. That is, the solution $\{c, x, \omega\}$ of Equations (III.15), (III.16) and (III.17) is unique.*

Proof. It is convenient to work out the proof by establishing the uniqueness of solution $\{x, \omega\}$ of equations (III.34) and (III.35), which is obtained by eliminating c from (III.15), (III.16), and (III.17). The domain on which the equations are to be considered is naturally the set of all nonnegative vectors x and scalars ω.

To this end, first define a mapping $K : R_+^n \longrightarrow R^n$ by

$$K(x) = x - (I - A)^{-1} G(p, \pi_1 x_1, \pi_2 x_2, \ldots, \pi_n x_n),$$

$$(\text{III.48})$$

then rearrange Equation (III.35) as

$$K(x) = (I - A)^{-1} \{F(p, 1) + \omega d\}. \qquad (\text{III.49})$$

The Jacobian matrix $J_K(x)$ of the mapping K can be similarly evaluated as in the preceding theorem, obtaining

$$J_K(x) = I - (I - A)^{-1} \left(\frac{\partial G_i}{\partial s_j}\right) \begin{pmatrix} \pi_1 & & 0 \\ & \pi_2 & \\ & & \ddots \\ 0 & & \pi_n \end{pmatrix} \qquad (\text{III.50})$$

where I is the identity matrix of the nth order. $J_K(x)$ is the identity matrix minus a nonnegative matrix at every x of R_+^n, since $(\partial G_i/\partial s_j)$ is nonnegative by virtue of the hypothesis of no inferior goods.

Next, in the light of (III.37) ensured by the hypothesis of no-greater-than-one marginal propensities to spend, one has

$$p'\left(\frac{\partial G_i}{\partial s_j}\right) \leqq (1, 1, \ldots, 1), \tag{III.51}$$

$$p'\left(\frac{\partial G_i}{\partial s_j}\right)\begin{pmatrix} \pi_1 & & 0 \\ & \pi_2 & \\ & & \ddots & \\ 0 & & & \pi_n \end{pmatrix} \leqq \pi' \tag{III.52}$$

instead of (III.44) and (III.45) in the preceding theorem. Therefore, by taking the definition of σ in (II.4) and (II.11) as well as (III.52) into account, one can see

$$(l + \pi)' J_K(x)$$

$$= l' + \pi' - (l + \pi)'(I - A)^{-1}\left(\frac{\partial G_i}{\partial s_j}\right)\begin{pmatrix} \pi_1 & & 0 \\ & \pi_2 & \\ & & \ddots & \\ 0 & & & \pi_n \end{pmatrix}$$

$$= l' + \pi' - p'\left(\frac{\partial G_i}{\partial s_j}\right)\begin{pmatrix} \pi_1 & & 0 \\ & \pi_2 & \\ & & \ddots & \\ 0 & & & \pi_n \end{pmatrix}$$

$$\geqq l' + \pi' - \pi'$$

$$= l' > 0',$$

that is,

$$\begin{cases} (l + \pi)' J_K(x) \geqq l' > 0' \\ l + \pi > 0, \end{cases} \tag{III.53}$$

a counterpart of (III.47).

Since $J_K(x)$ has all its offdiagonal elements nonpositive, as was seen above, (III.53) implies by virtue of the Hawkins-Simon's result [10] that all the principal minors of $J_K(x)$ are positive on R_+^n, a rectangular region. Therefore, the mapping K is univalent on R_+^n again by the theorem, already referred to in the proof of Theorem 6, due to Gale and myself. Therefore, the mapping has an inverse mapping K^{-1}: $K(R_+^n) \longrightarrow R_+^n$.

Moreover, this inverse mapping is monotonically increasing by virtue of another related theorem on a mapping with its Jacobian matrix having all offdiagonal elements nonpositive due to Gale and myself ([9], Theorem 5; Nikaido [18], Theorem 20.6, p. 373). Here the monotonic increasingness means that

$$K^{-1}(y^1) \geq K^{-1}(y^2) \tag{III.54}$$

for $y^1, y^2 \in K(R_+^n)$, $y^1 \geq y^2$.

Now, suppose that there are two distinct solutions $\{x^1, \omega^1\}$ and $\{x^2, \omega^2\}$ of Equations (III.34) and (III.35). They satisfy Equation (III.49), so that

$$K(x^t) = (I - A)^{-1} \{F(p, 1) + \omega^t d\} \quad (t = 1, 2). \tag{III.55}$$

Then, ω^1 and ω^2 must be distinct. For otherwise, $x^1 = x^2$ by (III.55) and the univalence of K, contradicting $\{x^1, \omega^1\} \neq \{x^2, \omega^2\}$. Hence, without loss of generality, it may be assumed that

$$\omega^1 > \omega^2. \tag{III.56}$$

(III.56) implies

$$(I - A)^{-1} \{F(p, 1) + \omega^1 d\} \geq (I - A)^{-1} \{F(p, 1) + \omega^2 d\},$$

$$\tag{III.57}$$

which entails by virtue of the monotonic increasingness of K^{-1}

$$x^1 = K^{-1}(y^1) \geq K^{-1}(y^2) = x^2 \qquad \text{(III.58)}$$

where

$$y^t = (I - A)^{-1} \{F(p, 1) + \omega^t d\} \, (t = 1, 2). \qquad \text{(III.59)}$$

Then, (III.56), (III.58) and the hypothesis of no inferior goods imply, because of the positivity of σ,

$$\sigma' \{\omega^1 d + G(p, \pi_1 x_1^1, \pi_2 x_2^1, \ldots, \pi_n x_n^1)\}$$
$$> \sigma' \{\omega^2 d + G(p, \pi_1 x_1^2, \pi_2 x_2^2, \ldots, \pi_n x_n^2)\}. \qquad \text{(III.60)}$$

But (III.60) obviously contradicts that $\{x^t, \omega^t\}$ $(t = 1, 2)$ satisfy Equation (III.34). Q.E.D.

III.4 Objective demand functions

The construction of objective demand functions has already been worked out substantially in the three foregoing sections in Chapter III. Thus, in order to construct these functions I have only to put the preceding results in a restated form.

The construction can be done in similar ways for both Say's and Keynesian cases formulated in [B.2] in III.1. Therefore, I will discuss only the Say's case, while I will merely make additional remarks on the Keynesian case.

First of all it should be recalled that the prices p_i and the profits per unit output π_i are always related to each other by the basic equation (II.11). Moreover, only such prices have been and will be considered in this work that the profits per unit output π_i are nonnegative. The relevant independent variables are π_i, rather than the prices, which are functions of the former through Equation (II.11). The price vectors fill out a cone P with σ as its vertex, which is in general smaller than the cone obtained by translating the nonnegative orthant by σ. Therefore the independent variables of the objective demand functions to be constructed are the profits per unit output π_i, though the functions can be thought of as being defined on P.

Now, the behaviors of workers are embodied in the supply function of labor $L(p, 1)$ and the demand function for goods $F(p, 1)$ as set forth in (II.6) and (II.7). Likewise those of capitalists' households are embodied in the demand function for goods $G(p, s_1, s_2, \ldots, s_n)$ formulated in (III.1).

Given an arbitrary profit per unit output vector π, which is naturally nonnegative, then the price vector p is determined by Equation (II.11), and there are supply of labor $L(p, 1)$ and workers' demand for goods $F(p, 1)$. After $F(p, 1)$, which is to be paid out as wages, is deducted, a possibility set of final demand vectors $C(\pi)$ and its efficient frontier $\Gamma(\pi)$ are left open to the capitalist class. There exist at least one competitive choice of a final demand vector c from among $\Gamma(\pi)$ and the corresponding gross output vector x by virtue of the results in III.2. Moreover, they are uniquely determinate by virtue of the results in III.3. Whence they can be thought of as single-valued functions $c(\pi)$ and $x(\pi)$ of the independent variable vector π. As was suggested, they may also be regarded as functions of the price vector defined on P, and $c(\pi)$ and $x(\pi)$ may alternatively be denoted by $c(p)$ and $x(p)$, respectively, if desirable.

This $x(\pi)$ is an objective *gross* demand function that has been sought for. The term gross means that the demand includes all derived demand $Ax(\pi)$. $x(\pi)$ is consistent with the complete circular flow of national income by commodity breakdown, as should be for an objective demand function.

The consistency immediately follows from the way in which $x(\pi)$ is constructed. In fact, there are sectoral profit incomes $\pi_i x_i(\pi)$ $(i = 1, 2, \ldots, n)$ at the price situation. These incomes induce effective demand for goods

$$G(p, \pi_1 x_1(\pi), \pi_2 x_2(\pi), \ldots, \pi_n x_n(\pi)), \qquad \text{(III.61)}$$

which also equal by construction $c(\pi)$. At the same time, there holds

$$x(\pi) = (I - A)^{-1} \{F(p, 1) + G(p, \pi_1 x_1(\pi), \pi_2 x_2(\pi),$$

$$\ldots, \pi_n x_n(\pi))\}, \qquad \text{(III.62)}$$

which shows a complete circular flow of national income guaranteed when production is carried out to meet the gross demand for goods $x(\pi)$.

There is a related consistency problem which was considered in I.3. In the above construction, the profit of the jth sector is $\pi_j x_j(\pi)$. Is this expression of profit equal to the total revenue less the total cost in the sector? The answer is affirmative and immediate. In fact, in view of the basic connection with the prices and the profits per unit output in Equation (II.11), one has

$$p_j x_j(\pi) - \sum_{i=1}^{n} a_{ij} p_i x_j(\pi) - l_j x_j(\pi)$$

$$= (p_j - \sum_{i=1}^{n} a_{ij} p_i - l_j) x_j(\pi) = \pi_j x_j(\pi)$$

$$(j = 1, 2, \ldots, n), \qquad \text{(III.63)}$$

where

$$p_j x_j(\pi) = \text{total revenue}$$

$$\sum_{i=1}^{n} a_{ij} p_i x_j(\pi) = \text{material cost}$$

$$l_j x_j(\pi) = \text{wages} \ (j = 1, 2, \ldots, n).$$

Thus all the consistency criteria are met by $x(\pi)$. It is noted that the equality of (III.61) to $c(\pi)$, (III.62) and (III.63) hold true identically at any π and the corresponding price vector p. Therefore, I should think that $x(\pi)$ can be regarded as an objective demand function. Incidentally, as is clear, the corresponding objective *net* demand function is

$$F(p, 1) + G(p, \pi_1 x_1 (\pi), \pi_2 x_2 (\pi), \ldots, \pi_n x_n (\pi)).$$

$$(III.64)$$

The economy is always in equilibrium at any π and the corresponding price situation in the sense that the market is cleared for each good. On the other hand, the price formation is effected by capitalists' control through more or less monopolistically competitive market structures, as will be considered in Chapters IV and VII.

Supplementary remarks on the Keynesian case are now in order. In this case, an investment composition vector d is given. d is a nonnegative vector having at least one component positive, and is either a constant or possibly a function of the price variables in general. Then, essentially the same reasoning as in the Say's case can apply to the Keynesian case, provided the scale of investment ω is regarded as a function $\omega(\pi)$ of π in addition to $c(\pi)$ and $x(\pi)$.

III.5 Objective demand functions—an example

In order to visualize objective demand functions, it is useful to have their specific shapes in an extremely simple, special situation. The construction of the functions is very easy. Nonetheless it is worthwhile noting that even in this simple situation their functional shapes are much different from those which the traditional oligopoly theorist has in mind.

The following example of objective demand functions will be given in the Leontief system of two goods and two sectors. Let the capitalist households' demand functions for goods in the Say's case be

$$G_i(p, s_1, s_2) = \frac{\beta_i(s_1 + s_2)}{p_i} \quad (i = 1, 2), \qquad (III.65)$$

where β_i's are constants such that

$$\beta_1 + \beta_2 = 1, \quad \beta_i > 0 \quad (i = 1, 2).$$

It is well known that (III.65) is derived from maximizing an additive logarithmic utility function subject to the budget constraint. It is well known that (III.65) satisfies gross substitutability

$$\frac{\partial G_i}{\partial p_j} \geq 0 \quad (i \neq j).$$

On the other hand, (III.65) satisfies all the assumptions set forth in the preceding sections, including the hypothesis of no inferior goods.

The uniquely determinate final demand vector $c(\pi) = (c_i(\pi))$ in the competitive choice is the solution of the system of linear equations

$$c_i(\pi) = \frac{\beta_i \{ p_1 c_1(\pi) + p_2 c_2(\pi) \}}{p_i} \quad (i = 1, 2) \tag{III.66}$$

$$\sigma_1 c_1(\pi) + \sigma_2 c_2(\pi) = M(\pi) \tag{III.67}$$

since the competitive choice must satisfy

$$\pi_1 x_1(\pi) + \pi_2 x_2(\pi) = p_1 c_1(\pi) + p_2 c_2(\pi). \tag{III.68}$$

The two equations in (III.66) are essentially identical, so that the system of equations determining $c_i(\pi)$ reduces to

$$\begin{cases} \beta_2 p_1 c_1(\pi) - \beta_1 p_2 c_2(\pi) = 0 \\ \sigma_1 c_1(\pi) + \sigma_2 c_2(\pi) = M(\pi). \end{cases} \tag{III.69}$$

The solution of (III.69) is

$$\begin{cases} c_1(\pi) = \dfrac{\beta_1 M(\pi)}{\beta_1 \sigma_1 + \beta_2 \sigma_2 (p_1/p_2)} \\[4mm] c_2(\pi) = \dfrac{\beta_2 M(\pi)}{\beta_1 \sigma_1 (p_2/p_1) + \beta_2 \sigma_2} \end{cases} \tag{III.70}$$

The total profit can be evaluated from (III.68) and (III.70) without evaluating $x_i(\pi)$. It is

$$\pi_1 x_1 + \pi_2 x_2 = \frac{M(\pi)}{\dfrac{\beta_1 \sigma_1}{p_1} + \dfrac{\beta_2 \sigma_2}{p_2}}. \tag{III.71}$$

Let specific forms of the workers' demand functions be given by

$$F_i(p, 1) = \frac{\alpha_i L(p, 1)}{p_i} \quad (i = 1, 2), \tag{III.72}$$

where α_i's are constants such that

$$\alpha_1 + \alpha_2 = 1, \alpha_i > 0 \quad (i = 1, 2)$$

and $L(p, 1)$ is the supply function of labor.

Then, in view of the definition of surplus value (II.15), one has

$$M(\pi) = \left\{ 1 - \left(\frac{\alpha_1 \sigma_1}{p_1} + \frac{\alpha_2 \sigma_2}{p_2} \right) \right\} L(p, 1). \tag{III.73}$$

From (III.70), (III.72) and (III.73) it follows that the objective net demand functions are

$$\begin{cases} F_1(p, 1) + c_1(\pi) = \dfrac{L(p, 1) \{\beta_1 p_2 + \sigma_2 (\alpha_1 \beta_2 - \alpha_2 \beta_1)\}}{\beta_2 \sigma_2 p_1 + \beta_1 \sigma_1 p_2} \\[3mm] F_2(p, 1) + c_2(\pi) = \dfrac{L(p, 1) \{\beta_2 p_1 + \sigma_1 (\alpha_2 \beta_1 - \alpha_1 \beta_2)\}}{\beta_2 \sigma_2 p_1 + \beta_1 \sigma_1 p_2} \end{cases}$$

$$\tag{III.74}$$

As was noted, π_1 and π_2 are independent variables, and p_1 and p_2 are linear functions of π_1 and π_2 by Equation (II.11) in (III.74). The set of all price vectors is a cone P with the labor value vector σ as its vertex, and a price vector p in P corresponding to a positive π is an interior point of P. In a small neighborhood of such an interior point the objective net demand functions (III.74) can be regarded as functions of independent variables p_1 and p_2 and need not and are most unlikely to satisfy gross substitutability provided $L(p, 1)$ is decreasing with respect to both variables p_1 and p_2, notwithstanding the gross substitutability of $F(p, 1)$ and $G(p, s_1, s_2)$ in the p_1 and p_2. The same remark still applies to a more specific situation where $\alpha_i = \beta_i$ $(i = 1, 2)$. The objective gross demand functions, which are linear functions of the objective net demand functions, are therefore most unlikely to satisfy gross substitutability. Moreover they need not be downward sloping even with respect to the price of the good in question. Accordingly, their functional behaviors diverge from what the traditional oligopoly theorist has in mind as to the shapes of demand functions.

III.6 Tâtonnement process for income formation

As was noted at the end of III.2, the determination of a competitive choice either by Equation (III.33) or by Equations (III.34) and (III.35) is the determination of the sectoral profit incomes $\pi_i x_i$ $(i = 1, 2, \ldots, n)$ of a Keynesian type at the rigid fixed price system. In the situation formulated by these equations, there are just x_i units of the gross demands for good i induced by the expected *ex ante* national income when the ith sector supplies x_i units of the gross output of good i in anticipation of the expected sectoral profit $\pi_i x_i (i = 1, 2, \ldots, n)$. If this mutual consistency of all the *ex ante* magnitudes is not instantaneously reached, but takes time, the income formation by these equations can be dynamized in the same way as in the usual multiplier process. For instance, the income formation by Equation (III.33) in the Say's case can be dynamized to a dynamic process formulated by the system of differential equations

$$\frac{dx_i}{dt} = \lambda_i Q_i(x) \quad (i = 1, 2, \ldots, n), \tag{III.75}$$

where

$Q_i(x)$ = the ith component of

$$(I - A)^{-1} \{F(p, 1) + G(p, \pi_1 x_1, \pi_2 x_2, \ldots, \pi_n x_n)\} - x$$

$$(i = 1, 2, \ldots, n) \quad \text{(III.76)}$$

λ_i = positive constant representing the speed of adjustment

$$(i = 1, 2, \ldots, n).$$

The system of differential equations generates a solution $x(t)$, starting at an arbitrary gross output vector $x(0) = x^0$, which depicts the variation of the gross output vector over time under a rigid price system. This dynamic process could be thought of as a multiplier process. However, here it might rather be regarded as a tâtonnement toward the situation brought about by the competitive choice, since the full employment relationship $l'x(t) = L(p, 1)$, or what amounts to the same thing, $o'G(p, \pi_1 x_1(t), \ldots, \pi_n x_n(t)) = M(\pi)$, does not necessarily persist during the working out of the process over time.

The process (III.75) is automatically endowed with a much stronger stabilizing propensity under the basic assumptions premised in III.1–3. Explicitly,

Theorem 8. (Global stability in Say's case.) *For a given fixed nonnegative π, the system of differential equations (III.75) generates a solution $x(t)$, starting at an arbitrarily given gross output vector $x(o) = x^0$. Any such solution converges to the unique gross output vector $\hat{x}$ in the competitive choice as the time t tends to infinity.*

Proof. First of all, it is noted, without going into the detail, that the basic assumptions in III.1–3 enable the system (III.75) to satisfy certain regularity conditions such that it has a solution starting at an arbitrary x^0. It is also important in this connection that the solution can be continued indefinitely for all nonnegative time points, while retaining the nonnegativity of $x(t)$ over time. For $Q_i(x) \geq 0$ by construction whenever $x_i = 0$.

Now define a mapping $Q : R_+^n \longrightarrow R^n$ by the formula

$$Q(x) = (Q_i(x)) \tag{III.77}$$

on the basis of (III.76). Then, the Jacobian matrix $J_Q(x)$ of the mapping is given by

$$J_Q(x) = (I - A)^{-1} \left(\frac{\partial G_i}{\partial s_j}\right) \begin{pmatrix} \pi_1 & & 0 \\ & \pi_2 & \\ & & \ddots \\ 0 & & \pi_n \end{pmatrix} - I \tag{III.78}$$

where I is the identity matrix. $J_Q(x)$ is nothing but $J_K(x)$ in (III.50) multiplied by -1. The result (III.53) was proved for the Keynesian case, and the proof was based on (III.52) which came from (III.37). Here one has (III.43), a sharpened version of (III.37), in Say's case. In the light of the above remark, one obtains

$$\begin{cases} (l + \pi)' J_Q(x) = -l' < 0' \\ l + \pi > 0, \end{cases} \tag{III.79}$$

a counterpart of (III.53). Since $-J_Q(x)$ has all its offdiagonal elements nonpositive, (III.79) implies that $J_Q(x)$ has all its diagonal elements negative and a dominant diagonal with respect to weighted column sums with constant positive weights $l_i + \pi_i$ $(i = 1, 2, \ldots, n)$. Thus by virtue of a theorem[14] on global stability due to S. Karlin ([11], Ch. 9, Theorem 9.5.1), the value

$$V(x(t)) \tag{III.80}$$

of a Lyapunov function

$$V(x) = \sum_{i=1}^{n} \left(\frac{\pi_i + l_i}{\lambda_i}\right) |\lambda_i Q_i(x)| \tag{III.81}$$

evaluated at $x = x(t)$ admits a right-hand side derivative with

[14] I am indebted to H. Atsumi for calling my attention to this result of Karlin.

respect to time which is negative unless $x(t)$ satisfies

$$Q_i(x) = 0 \quad (i = 1, 2, \ldots, n). \tag{III.82}$$

Whence

$$\lim_{t \to +\infty} V(x(t)) = 0. \tag{III.83}$$

But, since there is just one solution of the system of equations (III.82) by virtue of Theorems 4 and 6 in III.2 and 3, formula (III.83) implies that $x(t)$ converges to the unique gross output vector $\hat{x}$ in the competitive choice because of the continuity of the Lyapunov function (III.81). This completes the proof.[15]   Q.E.D.

Analogous results hold in the Keynesian case, too. A corresponding process adjusts both output levels and scale of investment ω toward the equilibrium stably by dominant diagonal.[16]

---

[15]It is noted that the stability theorem of Karlin alone cannot imply the convergence of $x(t)$ to a single gross output vector in a competitive choice. The stability theorem, in conjunction with the existence (Theorem 4) and uniqueness (Theorem 6) of competitive choice, can establish this theorem.

[16]The adjustment process is formulated as

$$\frac{d\omega}{dt} = \lambda_0 Q_0(\omega, x)$$

$$\frac{dx_i}{dt} = \lambda_i Q_i(\omega, x) \quad (i = 1, 2, \ldots, n)$$

where

$$Q_0(\omega, x) = \pi' x - p' \left\{ \omega d + G(p, \pi_1 x_1, \pi_2 x_2, \ldots, \pi_n x_n) \right\}$$

$Q_i(\omega, x) =$ the ith component of

$$(I - A)^{-1} \left\{ F(p, 1) + \omega d + G(p, \pi_1 x_1, \pi_2 x_2, \ldots, \pi_n x_n) \right\} - x$$

$\lambda_i =$ positive constants representing the speed of adjustment $(i = 0, 1, \ldots, n)$.

The nonnegativity of solution $\omega(t)$, $x(t)$ is ensured by the specific forms of Q_i's. The Jacobian matrix of the system has all offdiagonal elements nonnegative by the basic assumptions, including the hypothesis of no-greater-than-one marginal propensities to spend (III.37), and a negative dominant diagonal with regard to column sums for such a constant weight vector $(\delta, l' + \pi')$ that the scalar δ is larger than but sufficiently close to 1. The solution converges to the competitive choice determined by (III.34) and (III.35) by virtue of similar stabilizing force as in the Say's case.

CHAPTER IV

Monopolistically Competitive Pricing Modes and the Objective Demand Functions

IV.1 Capitalists' behaviors as entrepreneurs

It is important to recall that the working of the economy, if its bare aspects are boldly viewed, relies heavily upon such a function of the market price mechanism as to regulate the supply of labor $L(p, 1)$ and the real wage bill by commodity breakdown $F(p, 1)$ necessary for the full employment thereof. Once the price system is determined in one way or another, the capitalist class can choose a final demand vector c from among the possibility set $C(\pi)$, whether or not the choice is made through the market price mechanism. Therefore the market price mechanism is indispensable for the economy to achieve at least the allocation of labor and the distribution of the resulting output between the working and capitalist classes.

If the choice of a final demand vector is made by the capitalist class through the market price mechanism, there will be uniquely determinate objective demand functions for goods, as is the case when the capitalists' households take the prices as given parameters and behave as competitive demanders for goods. As was discussed in the foregoing two chapters, the price system determines the surplus value $M(\pi)$, and the competitive choice of a final demand vector c from among $C(\pi) = \{c \mid c \geq 0, \sigma'c \leq M(\pi)\}$ merely allocates the same surplus value to the n goods.

However, even if the capitalists' households behave as price takers, the capitalists as entrepreneurs do behave more or less as price setters. The price system, while regulating the supply of labor and the demand for goods, is determined by their price-setting behaviors and the interactions thereof subject to certain constraints, including the objective demand functions. Along the objective demand schedules the markets of all the goods are always cleared. The more or less monopolistically competitive market structure will single out a point on the objective demand schedules.

The basic general view in this chapter has already been accounted for in I.6. The n sectors in this economy are assumed to be single entrepreneurial decision-making units, respectively. Each of these sectors is confronted with the determinate objective demand function $x_j(\pi)$ for its product. If the sector is not deceived by any wrong perception but can see the bare situation that confronts it, its well-determinate profit is $\pi_j x_j(\pi)$, which is identically equal to the total revenue minus cost representation of the profit

$$
p_j x_j(\pi) - \sum_{i=1}^{n} a_{ij} p_i x_j(\pi) - l_j x_j(\pi),
$$

as was checked in III.4. Expressed in the terminology of game theory, here is a stage for an n-person game, with the profit $\pi_j x_j(\pi)$ as the payoff function of the jth player and the profit per unit output π_j as his strategy. Much of the interdependence of the n sectors is embodied in this formulation. Thus, a solution in game theory will narrow down the values of $\pi_j (j = 1, 2, \ldots, n)$ to a set, possibly to a single n-tuple, depending on the solution concept. Expressed in the terminology of the traditional theories of monopolistic competition, here is an oligopolistic market. So a typical solution concept such as the oligopolistic market equilibrium of the Cournot type will be applied to it in order to single out specific values of π_j's.

It should be noted, however, that here the game situation. or the oligopolistic market is formulated in terms of the objective demand functions, which are not so nicely shaped as game theorists and oligopoly theorists usually expect in their theories. In fact, the objective gross demand function for the jth good in the example in III.5 need not be downward sloping. Moreover, the profit $\pi_j x_j(\pi)$ is not necessarily a concave function. Therefore a theory of monopolistic competition in terms of objective demand functions has to challenge much of the arbitrary hypothesis setting in the traditional theories.

There might be various possible modes of capitalists' pricing, depending on the monopolistically competitive market structure. An extremely polar case is a joint maximization of the surplus value such as was discussed in II.3. Maximization of the surplus value singles out specific values of π_j's and hence p_j's, which brings about a situation of monopolistically competitive market equilibrium on the objective demand schedules. A maximum surplus value provides the capitalist class with the largest possibility set of final demand vectors $C(\pi)$, from whose efficient frontier a competitive choice of final demand vector is made at the corresponding price system (see II and III). Therefore joint surplus value maximization should be a virtue for the capitalist class, as far as the provision of goods in real terms is concerned. In the economy which is much cursed with the price mechanism, however, even the capitalist class is most likely to be unaware of the evaluation in terms of the labor value that prevails beneath the interplay of prices. Capitalists are concerned with profits, rather than surplus value. Therefore another more likely joint optimization may be joint profit maximization, which will be discussed in the following section.

In a joint optimization, capitalists form a special coalition, namely, that consisting of all of them. Coalitions of some of them are conceivable, and a game theory may be developed in terms of the core concept based on the coalition formation by sectors. But one must face difficulties in this line of theory-building. For there are many pecuniary externalities in connection with a coalition unlike the well-known core story about allocations brought about by competitive equilibria. A coalition in the story can enjoy an autarchy by taking advantage of an additive effect of the total resources of its participants, without being influenced by any externalities, just because the total resources of the economy are decomposable. This is not the case with the present situation. For the sectoral profit $\pi_j x_j(\pi)$ depends not only on π_j but also on the other π_j's. If the first and second sectors form a coalition, the sum of their profits $\pi_1 x_1(\pi) + \pi_2 x_2(\pi)$ is at the mercy of the capitalists outside the coalition. The formation of a coalition by some, but not all, of sectors seems to be impossible. But this is only a rough impression and needs a further careful study, which is beyond the present scope of this work.

If sectors' pricing behaviors are based on perceived demand schedules, yet another type of monopolistically competitive equilibrium, which may be called the Cournot-Negishi solution, is conceivable. The Cournot-Negishi solution is a specific n-tuple of π_j's such that at the corresponding points of the objective demand schedules the sectoral profits calculated in terms of the perceived demand schedules are maximized, respectively. The Cournot-Negishi solution will be discussed in IV.3.

IV.2 Joint profit maximization

In this monopolistically competitive economy in which everything is interdependent, profit maximization need not be a virtue, as far as satisfaction in real terms is concerned. The capitalist class could be better off by making surplus value larger, rather than profits, as was pointed out before. Nonetheless, capitalists almost always stick to profit maximization, either cooperatively or noncooperatively.

There is a possibility, however, that profits can be made indefinitely larger by charging higher profits per units of output and hence higher prices, while satisfaction resulting from the final demand vector chosen is decreasing. Capitalists are likely to seek a nominally larger profit at the cost of having a smaller possibility set of final demand vectors $C(\pi)$.

The values of sectoral profits $\pi_j x_j (\pi)$ may vary, as π_j's vary over all the nonnegative values. It ultimately hinges on the behavior of the supply function of labor $L(p, 1)$ whether the sectoral profits are bounded or not. For $x_j(\pi)$'s must satisfy by construction the equation $\Sigma l_j x_j(\pi) = L(p, 1)$, so that $x_j(\pi)$'s, which are nonnegative, are bounded and eventually tend to zero with $L(p, 1)$ as any of π_j's tends to infinity. Therefore the boundedness in question depends on how rapidly $x_j(\pi)$'s approach zero in relation to the growing π_j's.

The above remark suggests that maximum profits, sectoral or aggregate, can possibly be infinite under circumstances. It is recalled that a maximum surplus value exists under fairly weak conditions on $L(p, 1)$, as was seen in Theorem 2. But finite maximum profits may exist only when $L(p, 1)$ is required to satisfy a more stringent condition. One such additional condition may be given in terms of the elasticity of the supply function of labor.

[A.6] $L(p, 1)$ is differentiable and its elasticity satisfies

$$\frac{\displaystyle\sum_{j=1}^{n} \frac{\partial L}{\partial p_j} p_j}{L} \leqq -\gamma < -1 \quad \text{(identically).} \tag{IV.1}$$

If $L = 0$, formula (IV.1) does not make sense. Therefore (IV.1) can be given in the rearranged form

$$\sum_{j=1}^{n} \frac{\partial L}{\partial p_j} p_j \leqq -\gamma L \quad \text{(identically)}$$

$$\gamma > 1. \tag{IV.2}$$

Now, if [A.6] is added to the set of assumptions [A.1] – [A.5], one has

Theorem 9. *If p and π are related by Equation (II.11) as before, then*

64

$$\lim_{\pi_j \to +\infty} \pi_j L(p, 1) = 0 \quad (j = 1, 2, \dots, n), \tag{IV.3}$$

irrespective of whatever behaviors the other π_i's $(i \neq j)$ may have.

Proof. First, it will be shown that

$$L(tp, 1) \leq t^{-\gamma} L(p, 1) \tag{IV.4}$$

for any scalar $t \geq 1$. To this end, define

$$f(t) = L(tp, 1).$$

Then, upon differentiation and using (IV.2), one sees

$$f'(t) \leq -\frac{\gamma f(t)}{t}. \tag{IV.5}$$

First consider the case where $f(1) > 0$. Letting

$$g(t) = \frac{f(t)}{t^{-\gamma} f(1)} \tag{IV.6}$$

and using (IV.5), one obtains

$$g'(t) \leq 0. \tag{IV.7}$$

(IV.7) implies that $g(t)$ is nonincreasing, so that

$$g(t) \leq g(1) = 1 \quad (t \geq 1). \tag{IV.8}$$

In the light of the definitions of $f(t)$ and $g(t)$, inequality (IV.8) is nothing but (IV.4).

Now, (IV.5) implies that $f'(t)$ is nonpositive because $f(t) \geq 0$. Hence $f(t)$ is nonincreasing. Thus, if $f(1) = 0$, then

$$f(t) \leq f(1) = 0 = t^{-\gamma} f(1) \quad (t \geq 1). \tag{IV.9}$$

(IV.9) is again nothing but (IV.4).

Now, as π varies in such a way that $\pi_j \longrightarrow +\infty$ for any fixed j, one sees for $\pi_j \geq 1$

$$\pi_j L(p, 1) = \pi_j L(\pi_j (p/\pi_j), 1) \leq \pi_j^{1-\gamma} L(p/\pi_j, 1). \quad \text{(IV.10)}$$

The right-hand side of (IV.10) tends to zero as π_j tends to infinity, because of $\gamma > 1$ and the known boundedness of $L(p, 1)$. This completes the proof.   Q.E.D.

Theorem 9 immediately implies

Theorem 10. *If the input coefficients matrix A is explicitly assumed to be indecomposable, then*

$$\lim \pi_j x_j(\pi) = 0 \quad (j = 1, 2, \ldots, n)$$

as at least any one π_k of the π_j's tends to infinity.

Proof. It is noted that the objective gross demand functions $x_j(\pi)$ $(j = 1, 2, \ldots, n)$ satisfy

$$\sum_{j=1}^{n} l_j x_j(\pi) = L(p, 1) \qquad\qquad\qquad \text{(IV.11)}$$

identically for all π. Then, by (IV.11) and the nonnegativity of $l_j x_j(\pi)$, one obtains

$$\sum_{j=1}^{n} \pi_j x_j(\pi) = \sum_{j=1}^{n} (\pi_j/l_j) \, l_j x_j(\pi)$$

$$\qquad\qquad\qquad\qquad\qquad\qquad \text{(IV.12)}$$

$$\leq \sum_{j=1}^{n} (\pi_j/l_j) L(p, 1).$$

Now, $L(p, 1)$ tends to zero as the behavior of π stated above proceeds, because of the indecomposability of A and the basic assumptions on $L(p, 1)$.[17] Hence the jth term on the right-hand side of (IV.12)

[17]See (II.20).

$$(\pi_j/l_j) L(p, 1)$$

tends to zero by the convergence of $L(p, 1)$ to zero for bounded π_j's, and by Theorem 9 for unbounded π_j's. Therefore, the both sides of (IV.12) tend to zero. This proves the theorem, since $\pi_j x_j (\pi)$ are nonnegative.   Q.E.D.

Theorem 11. *There exists a positive maximum aggregate profit subject to the objective demand functions.*

Proof. By virtue of Theorem 10, the aggregate profit tends to zero if any of π_j's tends to infinity. On the other hand $x(0) \geq 0$ from (II.12) in assumption [A.5], so that $\pi' x (\pi) > 0$ for a small positive π by continuity. Thus the existence of a positive maximum of $\pi' x (\pi)$ over all π's can be proved in the same way as in the proof of Theorem 2.

                                                                Q.E.D.

If the profit of the jth sector is measured along the jth axis in the n-dimensional Euclidean space, the point

$$(\pi_1 x_1 (\pi), \pi_2 x_2 (\pi), \ldots, \pi_n x_n (\pi)) \qquad (\text{IV}.13)$$

fills out a set, as the profit per unit output vector π varies over all nonnegative vectors. The set may be termed the profit set, and its optimal frontier is defined to be the set of all points of the form (IV.13) at which the profit of any sector can not be increased without some other sector's profit being decreased.

The profit set is bounded, since it lies in the nonnegative orthant and the sum of the coordinates of any point in the set does not exceed the maximum aggregate profit. The optimal frontier is naturally bounded as a subset of the profit set. It is nonempty, because it contains special optimal points at which the aggregate profit is maximized.

The π's whose corresponding points (IV.13) belong to the optimal frontier form a bounded set in the π space. Otherwise, there is a sequence $\{\pi^\nu\}$ such that the point

(IV.13) for $\pi = \pi^{\nu}$ belongs to the optimal frontier, while $\pi_{j\nu}$ tends to infinity with ν for at least one j. Then, $\pi_{j\nu} x_j(\pi^{\nu})$ converges to zero for all $j = 1, 2, \ldots, n$ by Theorem 10. As was noted in the proof of Theorem 11, $x(0) \geq 0$. Moreover, one has even $x(0) > 0$, provided the indecomposability of A is taken into explicit account.[18] Therefore $\pi_j^0 x_j(\pi^0) > 0$ at the same time for $j = 1, 2, \ldots, n$ for a small positive π^0. Consequently,

$$\pi_{j\nu} x_j(\pi^{\nu}) < \pi_j^0 x_j(\pi^0) \quad (j = 1, 2, \ldots, n) \tag{IV.14}$$

for sufficiently large ν. But (IV.14) contradicts the inclusion of the points (IV.13) in the optimal frontier for $\pi = \pi^{\nu}$ with large ν. The set of such π's must therefore be bounded.

IV.3 The Cournot-Negishi solution

The importance of the Negishi solution in the general equilibrium theory of monopolistic competition has been discussed in I.1 and I.3. His theory is a noncooperative game theoretic analysis of entrepreneurial behaviors, and therefore of a Cournot type. In [5], Cournot originated the by now standard noncooperative oligopoly theory. In the market he considered, each oligopolist tries to maximize his profit calculated in terms of the demand function for the product by solely controlling his output on the assumption that the outputs of the rivals are given. The Cournot solution is the determination of the output and price by the simultaneous realization of the noncooperative profit-maximizing behaviors of all the oligopolists. The demand function in Cournot's theory is allegedly an objective demand function, which entails no problem just because the theory is of a partial equilibrium nature.

Negishi [15] (and [16], Ch. 7) is rightly conscious of the subjective character of firms' perceived demand functions

---

[18] $(I - A)^{-1} > 0$ by indecomposability (for example, see Nikaido ([18], Theorem 7.4, p. 107; [19], Theorem 20.2, p. 137)). Hence $x(0) = (I - A)^{-1} F(\sigma, 1) > 0$.

(more exactly, inverse demand functions). In his world of *monopolistic competition each monopolist tries to maximize* the profit calculated in terms of a perceived inverse demand function. The perception is not completely arbitrary, but depends more or less on the current state of the economy. The Negishi solution is a general equilibrium situation where both the noncooperative profit-maximizing behaviors of all firms and the market equilibrium in the sense of equality of demand and supply for all goods are simultaneously realized. It goes without saying that, in the Negishi solution, the firms' expected maximum profits evaluated in terms of the perceived inverse demand functions coincide with the actual realized profits.

Recall, however, Lange's characterization of a monopolistically competitive market as distinct from a perfectly competitive market, which is given in the passages quoted in I.3. The Negishi solution is not completely in accordance with the characterization, in that "disequilibrium consists in excess demand or excess supply" in the economy except at the solution. This is due to the lack of objective demand functions, which represent the current objective state of the markets always and even when there is disequilibrium in such a sense that the simultaneous realization of profit maximizations is not achieved.

Now that the well determinate objective demand functions have been constructed, it is possible to reconsider the Negishi solution in the presence of these functions in more concordance with the characterization of Lange.

Suppose that each sector has a perceived inverse demand function, by which it perceives an inverse demand schedule representing the price of the product of the sector as a function of its output, depending on the current state of the market. Explicitly, let

$$q_j(p, x, y_j) \quad (j = 1, 2, \ldots, n) \tag{IV.15}$$

be the perceived inverse demand function of the *j*th sector, representing the expected price of the jth good, where

> p = current price vector
> x = current gross output vector
> y_j = planned gross output in the jth sector.

The perception is so compatible with the current state of the market that (IV.15) satisfies

$$p_j = q_j(p, x, x_j), \qquad\qquad\qquad\qquad \text{(IV.16)}$$

where p_j and x_j are the jth components of p and x, respectively. For simplicity's sake, the functions (IV.15) are assumed to be linear in y_j, that is

$$q_j(p, x, y_j) = p_j - \eta_j(p, x)(y_j - x_j)$$
$$(j = 1, 2, \ldots, n), \qquad \text{(IV.17)}$$

where $\eta_j(p, x)$ are functions defined for $p > 0$ and $x \geq 0$. In general, they are downward sloping, so that

$$\eta_j(p, x) > 0 \quad (j = 1, 2, \ldots, n). \qquad\qquad \text{(IV.18)}$$

However, when perfect competition prevails, (IV.18) may be replaced by

$$\eta_j(p, x) = 0 \quad (j = 1, 2, \ldots, n). \qquad\qquad \text{(IV.19)}$$

Now, in the presence of the objective gross demand function $x(\pi) = (x_j(\pi))$, the current state of the economy may be represented by $(p, x(\pi))$. This means that currently the gross output which is exactly equal to the current demand $x(\pi)$ is supplied. Whence the markets are always currently cleared.

The perceived inverse demand functions corresponding to the actual current state of the economy takes the form

$$q_j(p, x(\pi), y_j) \quad (j = 1, 2, \ldots, n). \qquad\qquad \text{(IV.20)}$$

Taking p and $x(\pi)$ as given data, the jth sector maximizes its expected profit

$$\{(1 - a_{jj})q_j (p, x(\pi), y_j) - \sum_{i \ne j} a_{ij}p_i - l_j\} y_j$$

$$(j = 1, 2, \ldots, n) \qquad \text{(IV.21)}$$

by controlling the planned output y_j.

It is noted that (IV.21) equals the actual profit $\pi_j x_j(\pi)$ when y_j is set equal to $x_j(\pi)$. Then, the Negishi solution is defined as such a situation that the jth sector's expected profit (IV.21) is a maximum over all nonnegative y_j at $y_j = x_j(\pi)$. Thereby the Negishi solution singles out specific values of π and the corresponding $x(\pi)$ and p as a monopolistically competitive equilibrium.

Theorem 12. *If $\eta_j(p, x)$ are continuous and $\eta_j(p, x(\pi))$ are bounded ($j = 1, 2, \ldots, n$), there exists a Negishi solution.*

Proof. For each j the function (IV.21) is quadratic in y_j, since (IV.17) and (IV.18) are assumed. The coefficient of the quadratic term in it is negative. (IV.21) vanishes at $y_j = 0$. On the other hand, the expression in the braces in (IV.21) equals π_j at $y_j = x_j(\pi)$. If $\pi_j = x_j(\pi) = 0$, then $y_j = 0$ is maximizing (IV.21) with the vanishing derivative of (IV.21). Otherwise the expression in the braces in (IV.21) vanishes at a positive value of y_j. Hence (IV.21) takes on an interior maximum at $y_j =$ a half of the positive value with its vanishing derivative. In conclusion, for any given $\pi \ge 0$ (IV.21) always takes a maximum at some nonnegative value of y_j, with the vanishing derivative.

Differentiating (IV.21) with respect to y_j and setting the derivative equal to zero, one gets

$$(1 - a_{jj}) q_j (p, x(\pi), y_j)$$

$$- \sum_{i=1} a_{ij}p_i = l_j + (a_{jj} - 1)y_j \frac{\partial}{\partial y_j} q_j (p, x(p), y_j)$$

$$(j = 1, 2, \ldots, n). \qquad \text{(IV.22)}$$

71

Therefore the Negishi solution is determined by the system of equations obtained by substituting $x_j(\pi)$ for y_j in (IV.22) and taking (IV.16) into account. That is

$$p_j - \sum_{i=1}^{n} a_{ij}p_i = l_j + (a_{jj} - 1)x_j(\pi)\frac{\partial}{\partial y_j} q_j(p, x(\pi), x_j(\pi))$$

$$(j = 1, 2, \ldots, n). \qquad \text{(IV.23)}$$

But (IV.23) reduces by the definition of π_j to

$$\pi_j = (a_{jj} - 1)x_j(\pi)\frac{\partial}{\partial y_j} q_j(p, x(\pi), x_j(\pi))$$

$$(j = 1, 2, \ldots, n), \qquad \text{(IV.24)}$$

which, in the light of (IV.17), becomes

$$\pi_j = (1 - a_{jj})\eta_j(p, x(\pi)) x_j(\pi)$$

$$(j = 1, 2, \ldots, n). \qquad \text{(IV.25)}$$

(IV.25) is the final form of the system of equations determining the Negishi solution, and the proof of existence of the solution will now be taken care of by the Brouwer fixed point theorem again. To this end define the mapping $\chi : R_+^n \longrightarrow R_+^n$ by the formula

$$\chi(\pi) = (\chi_j(\pi))$$

$$\chi_j(\pi) = \text{the right-hand side of (IV.25),} \qquad \text{(IV.26)}$$

where naturally p is determined by π through Equation (II.11).

$x_j(\pi)$ is bounded, as was noted. $\eta_j(p, x(\pi))$ is also bounded by assumption. Whence the image $\chi(R_+^n)$ of R_+^n under the mapping is bounded. Therefore one can enclose $\chi(R_+^n)$ in a sufficiently large compact convex subset Λ of R_+^n, be it a cube or a simplex. One can thereby obtain a continuous mapping $\chi : \Lambda \longrightarrow \Lambda$. By virtue of the Brouwer fixed point theorem there is a fixed point $\hat{\pi} = \chi(\hat{\pi})$, and $\hat{\pi}$ is a solution of (IV.25). This completes the proof.   Q.E.D.

On the other hand, if perfect competition prevails so that (IV.19) holds instead of (IV.18), the expected profit can be maximized over all y_j only for $\pi_j = 0$ and $p_j = \sigma_j$ ($j = 1, 2, \ldots, n$). This special situation of the Negishi solution can also be characterized by equation (IV.25).

Finally, it is just noted that a dynamic process of monopolistically competitive price formation will be

$$\frac{d\pi_j}{dt} = \xi_j \{(1 - a_{jj}) \, \eta_j \, (p, x(\pi)) \, x_j(\pi) - \pi_j\} \tag{IV.27}$$

ξ_j = positive constant representing the speed of adjustment   ($j = 1, 2, \ldots, n$).

This process (IV.27) is not a tâtonnement, but proceeds with the current market transactions subject to the objective demand functions. The process is set in motion by the expected profit-maximizing entrepreneurial behaviors. It can be reformulated in terms of a system of difference equations for discrete time. However, the stability property of the process (IV.27) has not yet been explored.

CHAPTER V

Welfare Aspects of the Price Mechanism

V.1. Potential resource allocations

As was elucidated in the preceding sections and emphasized especially in the opening part of IV.1, the working of the economy heavily relies upon such a function of the market price mechanism as to regulate the supply of labor $L(p, 1)$ and the real wage bill by commodity breakdown $F(p, 1)$ necessary for the full employment of all the labor supply. The market price mechanism is indispensable for the economy to achieve at least the allocation of labor and the distribution of the resulting output in terms of labor values between the working and capitalist classes as the wages $\sigma'F(p, 1)$ and the surplus value $M(\pi)$, whereas the competitive choice of a final demand vector c from among the capitalists' possibility set of final demand vectors $C(\pi) = \{c \mid c \geq 0, \sigma'c \leq M(\pi)\}$ merely allocates the same surplus value to the n goods.

Now that the basic framework of the working of the economy is brought to light, it is in order and of interest to see how the market price mechanism prevents the economy from achieving a potential Pareto efficiency state of resource allocation. To this end the economy is assumed to include $r + s$ agents, namely, r workers $\alpha = 1, 2, \ldots, r$, and s capitalists' households $\beta = 1, 2, \ldots, s$, each of which has a utility function of the neoclassical type. Thus the workers' supply function of labor $L(p, 1)$ and demand function for goods $F(p, 1)$ can be thought of as the aggregate magnitudes of individual supplies of labor and demands for goods derived from their utility maximizations subject to budget constraints in a given price situation p.

Explicitly, let

74

$$U^\alpha (f^\alpha, L^\alpha) \quad (\alpha = 1, 2, \ldots, r) \tag{V.1}$$

be the utility function of the αth worker defined for all n-dimensional final demand vectors $f^\alpha > 0$ and labor supply L^α subject to an upper bound $\overline{L}^\alpha > 0$, and

$$V^\beta (g^\beta) \quad (\beta = 1, 2, \ldots, s) \tag{V.2}$$

be the utility function of the βth capitalist's household defined for all n-dimensional final demand vectors $g^\beta \geq 0$.

The above assumptions imply that consumption of a final demand vector induces a utility to both kinds of agents, and that exertion of labor by a worker induces a disutility to him, but neither utility nor disutility to other agents, especially, to all capitalists' households. These utility functions are further assumed to have all the nice properties premised in the neoclassical theory of consumer's behaviors, including differentiability and monotonicity, which will be freely utilized without explicit references thereto.

The production possibilities are extremely simple in the Leontief system with labor as a unique primary factor of production. In fact, z being the nonnegative total final demand vector and L being the total supply of labor, z is producible if and only if it satisfies $\sigma' z \leq L$, where σ is the labor value vector as set forth before.

With all these preliminary remarks in mind, it is now clear that a resource allocation is achieved when workers supply and exert L^α units of labor service, receive final demand vectors f^α, and capitalists' households receive final demand vectors g^β, respectively, subject to

$$\sigma' \left(\sum_{\alpha=1}^{r} f^\alpha + \sum_{\beta=1}^{s} g^\beta \right) \leq \sum_{\alpha=1}^{r} L^\alpha. \tag{V.3}$$

Then, the corresponding utility levels of the agents are given by (V.1) and (V.2).

Among all these utility levels potential to the economy, a Pareto optimum is characterized, as usual, as such a state that no agent can be better off without some other agents becoming worse off.

V.2. Pareto inefficiency of the market price mechanism

In the presence of the market price mechanism a resource allocation is implemented by means of it with the total supply of labor $L(p, 1)$ and workers' total final demand vector $F(p, 1)$. Such an allocation is generally Pareto inefficient in the sense that all the agents can be better off by allocating resources in an alternative way, as will be shown below.

Theorem 13. *A resource allocation implemented by means of the market price mechanism is Pareto efficient if and only if the price vector p equals the labor value vector σ, and therefore the surplus value is zero.*

Proof. If $p = \sigma$ and the surplus value is zero, the profit per unit output π_j is zero in each sector. Therefore the corresponding gross output level x_j can be thought of as a profit maximizing one for the price vector $p = \sigma$ taken as given, with the maximum profit being zero. Thus, there are zero profit incomes, so that $g^\beta = 0$ ($\beta = 1, 2, \ldots, s$) can be regarded as utility maximizing final demand vectors of capitalists' households subject to the budget constraints. It goes without saying that workers' price-taking behaviors are integrated to the corresponding values of the labor supply function $L(\sigma, 1)$ and the demand function $F(\sigma, 1)$. This means that the economy *can be regarded* as being in a competitive equilibrium situation, which is a Pareto optimum, as is well known.

The "only if" part of the proof proceeds as follows. Consider a Pareto optimum situation in which the workers and capitalists share final demand vectors f^α and g^β, respectively, while the workers supply and exert L^α units of labor service.

The monotonicity of utility functions makes the equality version of (V.3) valid in any Pareto optimum. If we assume for simplicity that corner optima are ruled out, a Pareto optimum can be obtained by maximizing a weighted sum of utilities

$$\sum_{\alpha=1}^{r} \zeta_\alpha U^\alpha (f^\alpha, L^\alpha) + \sum_{\beta=1}^{s} \eta_\beta V^\beta (g^\beta) \qquad (V.4)$$

with some positive weights $\zeta_\alpha, \eta_\beta (\alpha = 1, 2, \ldots, r; \beta = 1, 2, \ldots, s)$ subject to

$$\sigma' \left(\sum_{\alpha=1}^{r} f^\alpha + \sum_{\beta=1}^{s} g^\beta \right) = \sum_{\alpha=1}^{r} L^\alpha. \qquad (V.5)$$

Consequently, the following necessary conditions for an interior maximum obtain

$$\zeta_\alpha \frac{\partial}{\partial f_i^\alpha} U^\alpha (f^\alpha, L^\alpha) = \lambda \sigma_i \quad \begin{pmatrix} \alpha = 1, 2, \ldots, r \\ i = 1, 2, \ldots, n \end{pmatrix} \qquad (V.6)$$

$$\eta_\beta \frac{\partial}{\partial g_i^\beta} V^\beta (g^\beta) = \lambda \sigma_i \quad \begin{pmatrix} \beta = 1, 2, \ldots, s \\ i = 1, 2, \ldots, n \end{pmatrix} \qquad (V.7)$$

$$\zeta_\alpha \frac{\partial}{\partial L^\alpha} U^\alpha (f^\alpha, L^\alpha) = -\lambda \quad (\alpha = 1, 2, \ldots, r) \qquad (V.8)$$

where λ is a Lagrangian multiplier.

It follows from (V.6) and (V.8) that

$$\frac{\partial}{\partial f_i^\alpha} U^\alpha (f^\alpha, L^\alpha) \Big/ - \frac{\partial}{\partial L^\alpha} U^\alpha (f^\alpha, L^\alpha) = \sigma_i$$

$$\begin{pmatrix} \alpha = 1, 2, \ldots, r \\ i = 1, 2, \ldots, n \end{pmatrix}, \qquad (V.9)$$

which means that the ratio of the marginal utility of every

77

good to the marginal disutility of labor equals the labor value of the good for every worker. A Pareto optimum must satisfy (V.9).

Consider now a resource allocation implemented by the market price mechanism in which workers' and capitalists' households share final demand vectors f^α and g^β, respectively, and workers supply L^α units of labor service. Then, the pair (f^α, L^α) is maximizing the utility of the αth worker subject to the budget constraints

$$p'f^\alpha = L^\alpha, \qquad (V.10)$$

whence it must satisfy

$$\frac{\partial}{\partial f_i^\alpha} U^\alpha (f^\alpha, L^\alpha) \bigg/ - \frac{\partial}{\partial L^\alpha} U^\alpha (f^\alpha, L^\alpha) = p_i$$

$$\begin{pmatrix} \alpha = 1, 2, \ldots, r \\ i = 1, 2, \ldots, n \end{pmatrix}. \qquad (V.11)$$

Generally, (V.11) invalidates (V.9), and therefore a resource allocation implemented by the market price mechanism is not a Pareto optimum state, when the prices diverge from the labor values. (V.11) validates and reduces to (V.9) only when the prices equal the labor values, $p = \sigma$.   Q.E.D.

Theorem 13 has brought to light the fact that the presence of positive profits always gives rise to Pareto inefficiency via the market price mechanism in this economy, even though profit margins are charged at equal markup rates, so that the prices are proportional to the marginal costs and consumers' rates of substitution of goods equal those of technological substitution. It should also be noted that the assertion and derivation of Theorem 13 are firmly founded on the elucidation of the economy-wide framework of the economy's working, unlike the conventional partial equilibrium theoretic discussion of Pareto efficiency by welfare economists for economies whose overall workings they do not elucidate except for perfectly competitive ones.

A few words about the Marxian law of value seem to be in order. Consider a situation where good prices are proportional to their labor values σ_i, so that

$$\frac{p_i}{\sigma_i} = \rho \quad (i = 1, 2, \ldots, n). \tag{V.12}$$

Then, in the light of the workers' basic spending pattern $p'F(p, w) = wL(p, w)$ (Equation (II.8)), (V.12) implies

$$\frac{p_1}{\sigma_1} = \frac{p_2}{\sigma_2} = \ldots = \frac{p_n}{\sigma_n} = \frac{1}{[\sigma'F(p, 1)/L(p, 1)]}. \tag{V.13}$$

On the rightmost side of (V.13) there is

$\sigma'F(p, 1)$ = total wages in terms of labor values
= necessary amount of labor to reproduce $L(p, 1)$ units of labor in the Marxian terminology,

whence we have the wage rate 1, i.e., the price of labor, as nominator and the necessary amount of labor to reproduce one unit of labor as denominator. (V.13) is therefore the Marxian law of value, which means proportionality of goods' exchange values (Vertauschwert) to their labor values, including labor as a good.

V.3. Diagrammatic discussion

Theorem 13 can be vividly visualized for the simplest one good-one worker-one capitalist case on a diagram. To this end, let us measure labor service on the horizontal axis and the net output of the single good on the vertical axis in Figure 4. $\bar{L}$ is the least upper bound of the worker's possible labor supply. The straight line OA is the society's transformation curve and has the reciprocal of the labor value of the good as its slope.

Now, if the worker's share in the final demand is measured in the positive direction of the vertical axis starting on the horizontal axis, but that of the capitalist is measured in the negative direction of the vertical axis starting on the line OA, a point in the triangular region $O\overline{L}A$, a variant of the Edgeworth-Bowley box diagram, represents the society's resource allocation and allotment of the product to both agents.

Here, upward sloping curves are the worker's indifference curves, while straight lines parallel to OA are the capitalist's indifference curves. The contract curve, i.e. the set of Pareto optima, is the curve PQ. But the worker's offer curve is the curve PMR. The unique common point of both curves is P, which corresponds to the state of no profit, the only possible Pareto optimum reached through the price mechanism.

The price mechanism can implement any resource allocation corresponding to a point on the worker's offer curve by setting up a specific price of the good generally different from its labor value. In particular, a maximum surplus value discussed in Chapter II is reached somewhere on the worker's offer curve, say, at a point M, which is maximizing the capitalist's utility on the offer curve. Clearly, Figure 4 is a counterpart, in a situation involving production, of the unilateral monopoly solution in the pure exchange of two goods by two traders.

The discussion of a situation involving production as illustrated by Figure 4 seems to have been lacking in the economic literature,[19] while the unilateral monopoly solution in the pure exchange of two goods by two traders is too frequently discussed. This is almost unbelievable, all the more as monopoly emerges typically in a situation involving production. Whenever it comes to the analysis of a situation involving production, they lose the general equilibrium theo-

[19]Quite recently a few authors have been envisaging the general equilibrium theoretic aspects of monopolistic competition with special regard to interdependence in the objective sense as put forward in I.2 and I.3 in this volume. They are Cornwall [4] and Gabszewicz and Vial [7].

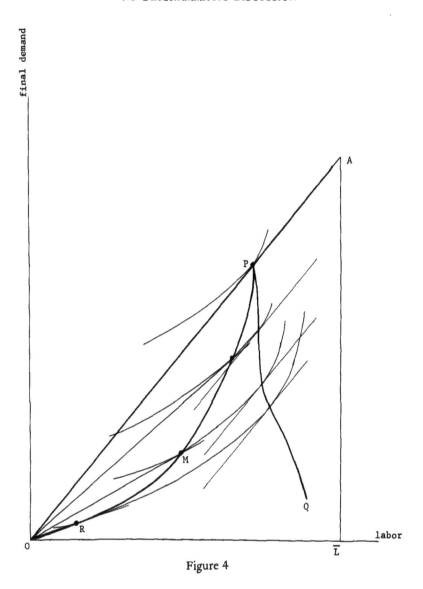

Figure 4

retic perspective and indulge in the partial equilibrium theoretic marginal-revenue-equals-marginal-cost argument in terms of a perceived demand function.

In Figure 4 the worker's offer curve is an *objective* framework to which the resource allocation implemented by the price mechanism is subjected irrespective of whether the capitalist envisages it correctly or not. A final solution always occurs somewhere in the framework, depending on one of the capitalist's alternative behavioral principles. The results in the preceding sections are intended to elucidate such an economy-wide objective framework of interdependence of all agents via the market price mechanism in a general many-good/many-agent version of the situation as illustrated in Figure 4 that it is always at work prior to any correct or wrong perceptions of the agents about it. The framework must be envisaged whenever one talks about the income distribution aspects of a national economy.

CHAPTER VI

Objective Demand Functions in the Presence of Capacity Limits

VI.1. Production capacity limits and surplus value, potential and utilized

It has been assumed in the foregoing analysis that only labor, the unique primary factor of production, is binding in the economy's production activities. The results in the preceding chapters remain valid even in the presence of production capacity limits, so long as there are idle excess capacities, with only labor being a binding factor.

Nonetheless, other capacity limits can possibly be binding sometimes, while labor becomes redundant. This chapter reconsiders the construction of objective demand functions worked out on the assumption of a single binding factor, labor, in Chapter III, so as to reconstruct them in the presence of effective binding capacity limits, including, naturally, labor.

In general, which capacity limits are binding hinges on the scale and composition of the specific bill of final demands to be produced. When there is unemployed labor due to some other binding capacity limits, the surplus value cannot be fully exploited by capitalists. This necessitates distinction of the surplus value *utilized* from the surplus value *potential*, which is necessary not for the sake of a Marxian-flavored metaphysical argument but as the first step toward the reconstruction of objective demand functions, the principal purpose of this chapter.

On the other hand I will not discuss where these capacity limits come from until I come to take into account fixed production equipment later in the following chapter.

It is recalled that Theorem 3, which amounts to asserting

Equation (III.7), i.e.

$$\pi'x(c) = M(\pi) - \sigma'c + p'c,$$

is instrumental in constructing objective demand functions for both cases, namely, J. B. Say's case and Keynesian case in Chapter III. The theorem is established on the full employment presumption, whose justification is discussed in II.4. It must and will be reformulated in accordance with possible underemployment of labor. To this end, the discussion in II.4 to justify the full employment presumption is a useful point of departure in this section.

Now suppose that the employment $l'x$ falls short of the supply of labor, while workers supply $L(p, 1)$ units of labor service and want to receive the final demand vector $F(p, 1)$. Then, assuming, as in II.4, that the wage bill by commodity breakdown paid out to the employed labor is $l'x/L(p, 1)$ times $F(p, 1)$, one sees that the capitalists' final demand vector $c \geq 0$ and the corresponding gross output vector $x \geq 0$ satisfy

$$x = Ax + \{l'x/L(p, 1)\} F(p, 1) + c \tag{II.26}$$

$$L(p, 1) \geq l'x \tag{II.27}$$

provided that $L(p, 1) > 0$.

(II.26) can be rewritten as

$$\left\{I - \left(A + \frac{F(p, 1)}{L(p, 1)} l'\right)\right\} x = c, \tag{II.28}$$

and it has been shown in II.4 that the coefficient matrix in (II.28) is invertible with a nonnegative inverse

$$\left\{I - \left(A + \frac{F(p, 1)}{L(p, 1)} l'\right)\right\}^{-1} \geq 0 \tag{VI.1}$$

if the surplus value $M(\pi)$ is positive, whereas it is singular, admitting

$$\sigma' \left\{ I - \left(A + \frac{F(p, 1)}{L(p, 1)} l' \right) \right\} = 0' \qquad \text{(VI.2)}$$

if $M(\pi) = 0$. Moreover, since the mode of wage payment, namely, either full $F(p, 1)$ or $\{l'x/L(p, 1)\} F(p, 1)$, does not affect the capitalists' possibility set of final demand vectors, as has also been shown in II.4, the following equation holds in the case (VI.1)

$$l' \left\{ I - \left(A + \frac{F(p, 1)}{L(p, 1)} l' \right) \right\}^{-1} = \lambda \sigma', \qquad \text{(VI.3)}$$

for the labor input vector l, the labor value vector σ and a positive scalar λ.

Theorem 14. *For any final demand vector c chosen by capitalists and the corresponding gross output vector x, which are characterized by (II.26), one has*

$$\frac{l'x}{L(p, 1)} = \frac{\sigma'c}{M(\pi)} \qquad \text{(VI.4)}$$

provided the surplus value $M(\pi)$ is positive.

Proof. x is determined by

$$x = \left\{ I - \left(A + \frac{F(p, 1)}{L(p, 1)} l' \right) \right\}^{-1} c, \qquad \text{(VI.5)}$$

whence

$$l'x = \lambda \sigma'c \qquad \text{(VI.6)}$$

in the light of (VI.3).

(VI.6) is valid whether or not the labor supply is fully employed. In a full employment situation $L(p, 1) = l'x$ and $M(\pi) = \sigma'c$, so that (VI.6) implies

$$L(p, 1) = \lambda M(\pi). \tag{VI.7}$$

Needless to say, (VI.7) is valid, whether or not labor is fully employed.

Now, using (VI.6) and (VI.7), one readily sees

$$\frac{l'x}{L(p, 1)} = \frac{\lambda\sigma'c}{L(p, 1)} = \frac{\sigma'c}{M(\pi)}$$

as was to be proved. Q.E.D.

If the labor supply $L(p, 1)$ cannot be fully employed but only a part of it $l'x$ is employed, the utilized surplus value $\sigma'c$ falls short of the potential surplus value $M(\pi)$, and (VI.4) means that the employment ratio equals the ratio of the utilized surplus value to the potential surplus value. More faithfully to the Marxian terminology, the ratio on the left-hand side of (VI.4) is that of the value actually produced to the value potentially producible, all evaluated in terms of labor values.

VI.2. Existence of a competitive choice, once again

It is now time to set out toward a reconstruction of objective demand functions in the presence of not only the limit of labor supply but also other capacity limits. However, the basic idea and notations will be the same *mutatis mutandis* as those in Chapter III, and the same methods of proof will be more carefully worked out.

It is recalled that the fundamental presumption in constructing the objective demand functions in Chapter III is the separation of the behaviors of capitalists' households as price-taking consumers from the price-setting behaviors of capitalists as entrepreneurs.

When the profit per unit output vector π is determined in some way, so that the price vector p is also given by Equation (II.11), the capitalists can pick up any final demand vector c from among their possibility set of final demand vectors

$C(\pi) = \{c \,|\, c \geq 0, M(\pi) \geq o'c\}$.   A competitive choice of a final demand vector c is defined in III.1 to be such a choice of c from among $C(\pi)$ that the corresponding profit incomes give rise to the effective demand, through aggregate demand functions of capitalists' households, for c that exactly clears the markets.

The aggregate demand function of capitalists' households $G(p, s_1, s_2, \ldots, s_n)$, an n-dimensional vector-valued function of the price vector p and the sectoral profit incomes s_j ($j = 1, 2, \ldots, n$) is classified in III.1 to two categories according to the spending pattern, namely, the J. B. Say type and Keynesian type. The average propensity to spend is one for the former, whereas it is less than one for the latter.

Now, in addition to the constraint on output by the limited supply of labor, capacity limits on it will be explicitly taken into account. Let

$$m_i > 0 \quad (i = 1, 2, \ldots, n) \tag{VI.8}$$

be the capacity limit of the ith sector's output x_i, and the capacity limit vector m be defined by

$$m = (m_i). \tag{VI.9}$$

The economy's production possibility is then constrained by the system of inequalities

$$\begin{cases} L(p, 1) \geq l'x \\ m \geq x. \end{cases} \tag{VI.10}$$

If $M(\pi)$ is positive, denoting the inverse matrix on the left-hand side of (VI.1) by E, one sees that the capitalists' possibility set of final demand vectors c at the *given price situation* is characterized by

$$\begin{cases} M(\pi) \geq o'c \\ m \geq Ec. \end{cases} \tag{VI.11}$$

When $M(\pi) = 0$, the first inequality in (VI.11) alone allows only $c = 0$ to be a unique possible final demand vector for capitalists.

Theorem 3 in III must and will be replaced by its counterpart, Theorem 15, in accordance with the new situation in question.

Theorem 15. *For any possible capitalists' final demand vector c, which need not satisfy the constraints (VI.11), and the corresponding gross output vector $x(c)$ determined by (II.26) (reproduced once again above), the relationship*

$$\pi'x(c) = p'c \qquad\qquad (VI.12)$$

holds. Here, the above c can be any nonnegative vector if $M(\pi) > 0$, whereas it is understood that $c = 0$ as a possible capitalists' final demand vector if $M(\pi) = 0$.

Proof. It is first noted that $x(c)$ is uniquely determined by c in (VI.5), if $M(\pi) > 0$. But $x(c)$ is indeterminate if $M(\pi) = 0$, because (II.26) becomes

$$\left\{I - \left(A + \frac{F(p, 1)}{L(p, 1)} l'\right)\right\} x = 0, \qquad\qquad (VI.13)$$

where the coefficient matrix is singular. In this case any nonnegative solution vector x of (VI.13) can be $x(c)$.

With the above remarks in mind, the proof will proceed as follows. In fact, the basic Equation (II.26) can be rewritten as

$$x = (I - A)^{-1} \left\{\frac{l'xF(p, 1)}{L(p, 1)} + c\right\}. \qquad\qquad (VI.14)$$

Premultiplication of (VI.14) by π' gives

$$\pi'x = \pi'(I - A)^{-1}\left\{\frac{l'xF(p, 1)}{L(p, 1)} + c\right\}$$

$$= (p' - \sigma')\left\{\frac{l'xF(p, 1)}{L(p, 1)} + c\right\}$$

$$= \frac{l'x(p' - \sigma')F(p, 1)}{L(p, 1)} + p'c - \sigma'c$$

$$= \frac{l'xM(\pi)}{L(p, 1)} + p'c - \sigma'c, \qquad\qquad \text{(VI.15)}$$

in the light of

$$\pi'(I - A)^{-1} = p' - \sigma'$$

$$M(\pi) = (p' - \sigma')F(p, 1),$$

the equations frequently utilized.
Now,

$$\text{the rightmost side of (VI.15)} = \begin{cases} p'c & \text{if } M(\pi) > 0 \\ 0 & \text{if } M(\pi) = 0 \end{cases}$$

by virtue of Theorem 14 and the understanding in the case of $M(\pi) = 0$. Q.E.D.

The difference of the results in Theorems 3 and 15 is due to the difference of the mode of wage payment. Labor always gets paid the full wage bill $F(p, 1)$ in physical terms independently of the level of employment in Theorem 3. Thus, part of the employed labor can possibly be laid off without wage cut, even if labor is fully employed but not fully utilized by the capitalists. On the other hand, only the amount of labor necessary to carry out production is employed and remunerated at the current wage rate in Theorem 15. It is noted, however, that both theorems amount to saying the same thing, when the labor supply is fully employed and utilized as in the situation in which the objective demand functions are constructed in III.

It is now in order to re-establish the existence of a competitive choice, a prerequisite to the reconstruction of objective demand functions, separately for both types of the capitalists' aggregate demand function $G(p, s_1, s_2, \ldots, s_n)$, the J. B. Say and Keynesian types. All the assumptions on G set forth in [B.1] and [B.2], III.1 will be retained here.

Theorem 16. (Existence of a competitive choice in Say's case, once again) *There exists a final demand vector c in the efficient frontier of the capitalists' possibility set of final demand vectors characterized by (VI.11) such that*

$$x(c) = Ax(c) + \{l'x(c)/L(p, 1)\} F(p, 1) + c \qquad (VI.16)$$

$$c = G(p, \pi_1 x_1(c), \pi_2 x_2(c), \ldots, \pi_n x_n(c)), \qquad (VI.17)$$

provided $L(p, 1) > 0$. Furthermore, the corresponding $x(c)$ must be on the efficient frontier of the economy's production possibility set constrained by (VI.10), if $M(\pi) > 0$. When $M(\pi) = 0$, $x(c)$ is indefinite, but can be chosen so as for it to lie on the efficient frontier.

Proof. The singular case $M(\pi) = 0$ will be discussed first. In this case $c = 0$ and any nonnegative solution vector x of Equation (VI.13) as a corresponding $x(c)$ form a solution of (VI.16) and (VI.17). This can be verified as follows. Clearly such a pair of vectors satisfies (VI.16). Next, by virtue of the spending of the entire profit incomes as set forth in [B.2] in III.1,

$$p'G(p, \pi_1 x_1(c), \pi_2 x_2(c), \ldots, \pi_n x_n(c))$$
$$= \pi'x(c) \qquad (VI.18)$$

which must be zero by Theorem 15. Then the positivity of p and the nonnegativity of G imply that the right-hand side of (VI.17) vanishes and therefore equals the left-hand side of

(VI.17) for $c = 0$, as was to be verified. Clearly this x can be chosen so as for it to lie on the efficient frontier.

Now, the normal case $M(\pi) > 0$ will be discussed. In this case $x(c)$ is uniquely determined for c through (VI.5) and is a continuous function of c.

Let T be the efficient frontier of the capitalists' possibility set of final demand vectors characterized by (VI.11). T is the set of all c for which not all of the component inequalities of (VI.11) are strict inequalities. In general T is not convex, but topologically equivalent to an $(n - 1)$-dimensional simplex; that is to say, the points of T can be put in one-to-one correspondence with those of the simplex in such a way that the correspondence is continuous in both directions. The Brouwer fixed point theorem still holds as well in T.

If the indecomposability of A is explicitly taken into account,

$$A + \frac{F(p, 1)}{L(p, 1)} l'$$

is also indecomposable, so that E is a positive matrix. Let $e'(i)$ $(i = 1, 2, \ldots, n)$ be the ith row vector of E. These vectors are positive, because E is positive.

Next let the function

$$\gamma(c) = \min \left[\frac{M(\pi)}{\sigma'G}, \frac{m_1}{e'(1)G}, \ldots, \frac{m_n}{e'(n)G} \right] \qquad \text{(VI.19)}$$

be defined on T, where G stands for

$$G(p, \pi_1 x_1 (c), \pi_2 x_2 (c), \ldots, \pi_n x_n (c)). \qquad \text{(VI.20)}$$

$\gamma(c)$ is well defined for the following reason. In fact, a vector c in T must be semi-positive, because equality holds for at least one component inequality of (VI.11). Then, $p'c > 0$ by the positivity of p, which ensures $\pi'x(c) > 0$ by Theorem 15. Consequently, one must have

$$p'G(p, \pi_1 x_1(c), \pi_2 x_2(c), \ldots, \pi_n x_n(c)) > 0 \qquad \text{(VI.21)}$$

in the light of (VI.18). Thus (VI.21), in conjunction with $p > 0$ and $G \geq 0$, implies $G \geq 0$. Since σ' and $e'(i)$ $(i = 1, 2, \ldots, n)$ are positive, the denominators in the brackets in (VI.19) are always positive for c in T, so that $\gamma(c)$ is a well-defined continuous function which always takes on a positive value.

Consider now the continuous mapping $\Phi : T \longrightarrow T$ defined by

$$\Phi(c) = \gamma(c) \, G(p, \pi_1 x_1(c), \ldots, \pi_n x_n(c)). \qquad \text{(VI.22)}$$

It is obvious by construction that Φ maps continuously T into T. Therefore, by virtue of the Brouwer fixed point theorem as applied to T, Φ has a fixed point $\hat{c}$ such that

$$\hat{c} = \Phi(\hat{c}) = \gamma(\hat{c}) \, G(p, \pi_1 x_1(\hat{c}), \ldots, \pi_n x_n(\hat{c})). \qquad \text{(VI.23)}$$

Premultiplication of (VI.23) by p' gives, in the light of (VI.12) in Theorem 15 and (VI.18) again,

$$p'\hat{c} = \gamma(\hat{c}) \, p'\hat{c}, \qquad \text{(VI.24)}$$

which implies

$$\gamma(\hat{c}) = 1$$

by the positivity of $p'\hat{c}$. Thus, (VI.23) reduces to (VI.17) for $c = \hat{c}$. (VI.16) holds for any c by construction and *a fortiori* for $c = \hat{c}$.

Finally, $x(c)$ always lies on the economy's efficient frontier at the given price system for any c in T, because $L(p, 1) = l'x(c)$ if and only if $M(\pi) = \sigma'c$ by Theorem 14 and because $x(c) = Ec$. Q.E.D.

Theorem 17. (Existence of a competitive choice in Keynesian case, once again) *Let $d \geq 0$ be a given investment composition vector which is constant. Then, there exist a* *final demand vector c and a nonnegative scalar ω such that*

$$\omega d + c \in T \tag{VI.25}$$

$$x = Ax + \{l'x/L(p, 1)\}\, F(p, 1) + \omega d + c \tag{VI.26}$$

$$c = G(p, \pi_1 x_1, \pi_2 x_2, \ldots, \pi_n x_n), \tag{VI.27}$$

provided $L(p, 1) > 0$, where T is the efficient frontier of the capitalists' possibility set of final demand vectors at the given price system. Furthermore, the x must be on the efficient frontier of the economy's production possibility set constrained by (VI.10), if $M(\pi) > 0$. When $M(\pi) = 0$, the x is indefinite, but can be chosen so as for it to lie on the efficient frontier. The ω is positive if and only if $M(\pi) > 0$.

Proof. It is recalled that the spending patterns of capitalists' households in the Keynesian case are formulated in [B.2] in III.1 in such a way that

$$p'G(p, \pi_1 x_1, \pi_2 x_2, \ldots, \pi_n x_n) \leqq \theta \pi' x, \tag{VI.28}$$

where θ is a positive constant less than one.

Moreover, it is noted that Theorem 15 holds for c replaced by $\omega d + c$ as well. Hence

$$\pi' x = p'(\omega d + c) \tag{VI.29}$$

for any $\omega \geqq 0$, $c \geqq$ and $x \geqq 0$ satisfying (VI.26).

The singular case $M(\pi) = 0$ can be discussed in essentially the same way as in the preceding theorem, obtaining a solution consisting of $\omega = 0$, $c = 0$ and an output vector x in the economy's efficient frontier that satisfies Equation (VI.13). (VI.2) rules out the existence of solutions of other types, so that ω must vanish.

To prove the case $M(\pi) > 0$, let the function

$$\omega(c) = \max \left[0, \min \left\{ \frac{M(\pi) - \sigma'c}{\sigma'd} , \right. \right.$$

$$\left. \left. \frac{m_1 - e'(1)c}{e'(1)d} , \ldots , \frac{m_n - e'(n)c}{e'(n)d} \right\} \right] \qquad \text{(VI.30)}$$

be defined for all $c \geq 0$, where

σ = the labor value vector

m_i = the ith component of the capacity limit vector m

$e'(i)$ = the ith row of the matrix E,

all of which are positive, as has been made clear. $\omega(c)$ is a well-defined continuous function of $c \geq 0$ and takes on non-negative values. It is also obvious from definition that

$$\omega(c) \leq \frac{M(\pi)}{\sigma'd} . \qquad \text{(VI.31)}$$

Now, let the continuous mapping $\Psi : R_+^n \longrightarrow R_+^n$ be defined by

$$\Psi(c) = G(p, \pi_1 x_1(c), \ldots, \pi_n x_n(c)) \qquad \text{(VI.32)}$$

$$x(c) = \left\{ I - \left(A + \frac{F(p, 1)}{L(p, 1)} l' \right) \right\}^{-1} (\omega(c)d + c), \qquad \text{(VI.33)}$$

where R_+^n is the nonnegative orthant.

Then, in view of (VI.28) and (VI.29), one has

$$p'\Psi(c) \leq \theta(\omega(c)p'd + p'c), \qquad \text{(VI.34)}$$

which implies in the light of (VI.31)

$$p'\Psi(c) \leq \frac{\theta p'dM(\pi)}{\sigma'd} + \theta p'c. \qquad \text{(VI.35)}$$

Hence Ψ can be contracted to a continuous mapping from a compact convex subset of R_+^n into itself by confining Ψ in exactly the same way as in the proof of Theorem 5 in III.2 to such a large simplex

$$\Delta = \{c \mid c \geq 0, \delta \geq p'c\}$$

that

$$\Delta \supset \Psi(\Omega),$$

where

$$\Omega = \left\{ c \mid c \geq 0, \frac{\theta p' dM(\pi)}{(1 - \theta)\sigma' d} \geq p'c \right\}.$$

The continuous mapping $\Psi : \Delta \longrightarrow \Delta$, therefore, has a fixed point $\hat{c}$ by virtue of the Brouwer fixed point theorem, and

$$\hat{c} = \Psi(\hat{c}). \tag{VI.36}$$

This $\hat{c}$ and the corresponding $\omega(\hat{c})$ clearly satisfy Equations (VI.26) and (VI.27). It still remains to show, however, that they satisfy (VI.25), with the corresponding $x(c)$ lying on the economy's efficient frontier. To this end, it suffices to see the positivity of $\omega(\hat{c})$. For, if $\omega(\hat{c}) > 0$, from definition (VI.30) it follows that all the inequalities

$$M(\pi) \geq \sigma'(\omega(\hat{c})d + \hat{c}), m_i \geq e'(i)(\omega(\hat{c})d + \hat{c})$$

$$(i = 1, 2, \ldots, n) \tag{VI.37}$$

hold, with strict equality holding for at least one of them.

Now suppose that $\omega(\hat{c}) = 0$. Then, (VI.34) and (VI.36) for $c = \hat{c}$ and $\omega(\hat{c}) = 0$ lead to

$$p'\hat{c} \leq \theta p'\hat{c}. \tag{VI.38}$$

But (VI.38) implies $\hat{c} = 0$, because $1 > \theta > 0$, $p > 0$, $\hat{c} \geq 0$. On the other hand, $\omega(0)$ must be positive from definition (VI.30), a contradiction. The existence of a competitive choice has thereby been proved. Since it is readily seen that any competitive choice must be a fixed point of Ψ for the case $M(\pi) > 0$, the arguments in the last parts of the proofs for both cases $M(\pi) = 0$ and $M(\pi) > 0$ have already established the assertion that ω is positive if and only if $M(\pi) > 0$.

Finally, the assertion about the efficiency of the corresponding x can be seen in essentially the same way as in the J. B. Say's case.   Q.E.D.

VI.3. Uniqueness of competitive choice, once again

The uniqueness of competitive choice can be proved in the presence of capacity limits along with the same idea of methods of proof based on the global univalence theorems of Gale and myself ([9]; [18], Ch. VII) as in Theorems 6 and 7 without capacity limits. However, the new situation necessitates more prudence in working out the proofs in this line. In fact, a direct application of the method of proof in Theorem 6 to the J. B. Say's case would lead to a serious difficulty, since the relevant Jacobian vanishes. More prudence is therefore needed, though the new situation can still be taken care of by the global univalence theorems.

It is useful in working out the proofs in the new situation to transform the relevant equations in terms of the final demand vector c as an independent variable to equations in terms of the gross output vector x as an independent variable not only for the Keynesian case but also for the Say's case.

The new equations are given below. First, the competitive choice in the Say's case can be reformulated as the determination of the gross output vector x by virtue of the equations

$$G(p, \pi_1 x_1, \pi_2 x_2, \ldots, \pi_n x_n) \in T, \tag{VI.39}$$

with x lying on the economy's efficient frontier   (VI.40)

$$x = Ax + \{l'x/L(p, 1)\} F(p, 1)$$
$$+ G(p, \pi_1 x_1, \pi_2 x_2, \ldots, \pi_n x_n). \tag{VI.41}$$

Second, the competitive choice in the Keynesian case can be reformulated as the determination of the gross output vector x and the scale of investment ω by means of the equations

$$\omega d + G(p, \pi_1 x_1, \pi_2 x_2, \ldots, \pi_n x_n) \in T, \qquad (VI.42)$$

with x lying on the economy's efficient frontier $\quad (VI.43)$

$$x = Ax + \{l'x/L(p, 1)\} F(p, 1)$$
$$+ \omega d + G(p, \pi_1 x_1, \pi_2 x_2, \ldots, \pi_n x_n). \qquad (VI.44)$$

Needless to say, the above equations are formulated on the assumption of positive labor supply $L(p, 1) > 0$, whereas the only possible solution is $x = 0$ if $L(p, 1) = 0$. They are counterparts of (III.33) for Say's case and (III.34) and (III.35) for Keynesian case, respectively.

It is recalled that the assumptions on the spending patterns of capitalists' households played an important role in establishing uniqueness in both Say's and Keynesian cases in III.3. One of them is the hypothesis of no inferior goods, as formulated in [B.3] in III.3, which means

$$\frac{\partial G_i}{\partial s_j} = G_{ij}(p, s_1, s_2, \ldots, s_n) \geqq 0 \quad (i, j = 1, 2, \ldots, n)$$

in Equation (III.36). This hypothesis will be retained as a basic assumption to secure uniqueness in the new situation.

The additional assumption of no-greater-than-one marginal propensities to spend, formulated in (III.37), which reinforced the hypothesis of no inferior goods in the proof of uniqueness for the Keynesian case, will be slightly strengthened to the assumption of less-than-one marginal propensities to spend, meaning

$$\sum_{i=1}^{n} p_i \frac{\partial G_i}{\partial s_j} < 1 \quad (j = 1, 2, \ldots, n). \qquad (VI.45)$$

It is remembered that less-than-one marginal propensities to spend are implied by the nonincreasing average propensity to spend and uniformly bounded by θ, as was remarked in III.3. At any rate, (VI.45) may be expressed as

$$\sum_{i=1}^{n} p_i \frac{\partial G_i}{\partial s_j} \leq \epsilon < 1 \quad (j = 1, 2, \ldots, n) \tag{VI.46}$$

by using a number ϵ common for all $j = 1, 2, \ldots n$, whether the less-than-one marginal propensities to spend have been derived from the nonincreasing average propensity to spend or not.

Finally, it is also noted that the indecomposability of the input coefficients matrix A will be explicitly taken into account and utilized in the proofs of both theorems below.

Theorem 18. (Uniqueness of competitive choice in Say's case, once again) *Under differentiability, if there are no inferior goods for the capitalist households, then the competitive choice is unique even in the presence of capacity limits. That is, the solution x of Equations (VI.39), (VI.40) and (VI.41) is unique.*

Proof. First, it is obvious that (VI.40) implies (VI.39), whence one has only to take (VI.40) and (VI.41) into account.

Next, let certain useful information be derived separately for both situations $M(\pi) = 0$ and $M(\pi) > 0$ from concentrating attention only to Equation (VI.41), ignoring (VI.40) for the moment and taking it again into consideration at the final step of the proof.

The singular situation $M(\pi) = 0$ can be discussed as follows. Equation (VI.41) can be rearranged to

$$\left\{ I - \left(A + \frac{F(p, 1)}{L(p, 1)} l' \right) \right\} x$$
$$= G(p, \pi_1 x_1, \ldots, \pi_n x_n) \tag{VI.47}$$

as in (II.28) (reproduced right above (VI.1)). Then, pre-multiplication of (VI.47) by σ' gives

$$\sigma' G(p, \pi_1 x_1, \pi_2 x_2, \ldots, \pi_n x_n) = 0 \qquad \text{(VI.48)}$$

because of (VI.2). (VI.48) implies that the right-hand side of (VI.47) must be zero, since $\sigma > 0$ and $G \geq 0$, so that (VI.47) turns out to be (VI.13), i.e.,

$$\left\{ I - \left(A + \frac{F(p, 1)}{L(p, 1)} l' \right) \right\} x = 0.$$

The above result means that the nonnegative vector x is either 0 or an eigenvector of the indecomposable nonnegative matrix

$$A + \frac{F(p, 1)}{L(p, 1)} l'$$

associated with its dominant eigenvalue 1. $x = 0$ is ruled out, since x must be on the economy's efficient frontier. Then, x must be positive and unique up to a positive scalar,[20] and therefore must also be uniquely determined so as for it to belong to the economy's efficient frontier.

The proof will now proceed to the situation $M(\pi) > 0$. The proof will be worked out along with the idea stated earlier. At the first step of the proof it is important to consider Equation (VI.41) on the entire nonnegative orthant, although the solution occurs only on the economy's efficient frontier.

Now let the mapping $U : R_+^n \longrightarrow R^n$ be defined by

$$U(x) = x - \{ Ax + G(p, \pi_1 x_1, \pi_2 x_2, \ldots, \pi_n x_n) \}.$$

$$\text{(VI.49)}$$

The Jacobian matrix $J_U(x)$ of the mapping is given by

---

[20] For example, see Nikaido ([18], Theorem 7.3, p. 107; [19], Theorem 20.1, p. 135).

$$J_U(x) = I - \left\{ A + \left(\frac{\partial G_i}{\partial s_j}\right) \begin{pmatrix} \pi_1 & & & 0 \\ & \pi_2 & & \\ & & \ddots & \\ 0 & & & \pi_n \end{pmatrix} \right\},$$

$$(VI.50)$$

where

$$\left(\frac{\partial G_i}{\partial s_j}\right) = \text{the Jacobian matrix of } G$$

$$\begin{pmatrix} \pi_1 & & & 0 \\ & \pi_2 & & \\ & & \ddots & \\ 0 & & & \pi_n \end{pmatrix} = \text{the diagonal matrix with } \pi_i \text{ on the principal diagonal.}$$

Then, it is readily seen, in the light of the price equation

$$p'(I - A) = l' + \pi'$$

and the unitary marginal propensities to spend

$$\sum_{i=1}^{n} p_i \frac{\partial G_i}{\partial s_j} = 1 \quad (j = 1, 2, \ldots, n)$$

implied by the full spending of profit incomes, that

$$p' J_U(x) = l' > 0. \tag{VI.51}$$

$J_U(x)$ has all its offdiagonal elements nonpositive, since the Jacobian matrix of G is nonnegative from the hypothesis of no inferior goods. Therefore the truth of Equation (VI.51) for the positive p and l implies by virtue of the Hawkins-Simon result [10] that all the principal minors of $J_U(x)$ are positive on R_+^n, a rectangular region. Consequently, the mapping U is univalent on R_+^n by the univalence theorem on a mapping having a P-Jacobian matrix due to Gale and myself ([9], Theorem 4; Nikaido [18], Theorem 20.4, p.

370). Moreover, the inverse mapping $U^{-1} : U(R_+^n) \longrightarrow R_+^n$ is monotonic-increasing by virtue of another related theorem on a mapping with its Jacobian matrix having all offdiagonal elements nonpositive also due to Gale and myself ([9], Theorem 5; Nikaido [18], Theorem 20.6, p. 373). The monotonic increasingness of U^{-1} means that

$$U^{-1}(y^1) \geq U^{-1}(y^2) \tag{VI.52}$$

for $y^1, y^2 \in U(R_+^n), y^1 \geq y^2$, as in (III.54) for K.

Now, Equation (VI.41) can be rearranged to

$$U(x) = \{l'x/L(p, 1)\} F(p, 1). \tag{VI.53}$$

Suppose that there are two distinct solutions x^1 and x^2. They satisfy (VI.53), so that

$$U(x^t) = \{l'x^t/L(p, 1)\} F(p, 1) \quad (t = 1, 2). \tag{VI.54}$$

They must also satisfy $l'x^1 \neq l'x^2$. For otherwise $x^1 = x^2$ from the univalence of U in (VI.54). Thus, it may be assumed without loss of generality that

$$l'x^1 > l'x^2. \tag{VI.55}$$

It is also noted that $F(p, 1) \geq 0$, since $p'F(p\ 1) = L(p, 1) > 0$, $p > 0$, and $F(p, 1) \geq 0$. If the right-hand sides of (VI.54) are denoted by y^1 and y^2 for $t = 1, 2$, respectively, the above result, in conjunction with (VI.55), implies $y^1 \geq y^2$. Hence

$$x^1 = U^{-1}(y^1) \geq U^{-1}(y^2) = x^2 \tag{VI.56}$$

by (VI.52).

Now that (VI.56) has been brought to light, let Equation (VI.41) be rearranged once more to another form, obtaining the expressions

$$x^t = (I - A)^{-1} \left\{ \frac{l'x^t}{L(p, 1)} F(p, 1) \right.$$

$$\left. + G(p, \pi_1 x_1^t, \ldots, \pi_n x_n^t) \right\} \quad (t = 1, 2). \quad \text{(VI.57)}$$

Then, in (VI.57) the inverse matrix of $I - A$ is positive because of indecomposability,[21] and

$$G(p, \pi_1 x_1^1, \ldots, \pi_n x_n^1) \geq G(p, \pi_1 x_1^2, \ldots, \pi_n x_n^2)$$

$$\text{(VI.58)}$$

by (VI.56) and the hypothesis of no inferior goods. Moreover,

$$F(p, 1) \geq 0 \qquad \qquad \text{(VI.59)}$$

as was pointed out above.

Now, (VI.55), (VI.58), (VI.59) and the positivity of the coefficient matrix in (VI.57) altogether give rise to

$$x^1 > x^2. \qquad \qquad \text{(VI.60)}$$

But (VI.60) means that one of x^1 and x^2 cannot lie on the economy's efficient frontier, contradicting (VI.40). This completes the proof.   Q.E.D.

Theorem 19. (Uniqueness of competitive choice in Keynesian case, once again.) *Under differentiability, if there are no inferior goods for the capitalist households, and if their marginal propensities to spend are less than one, then the competitive choice is unique even in the presence of capacity limits. That is, the solution $\{x, \omega\}$ of Equations (VI.42), (VI.43) and (VI.44) is unique.*

Proof. It is readily seen, as in the preceding theorem, that (VI.43) implies (VI.42). Moreover, the singular situation

---

[21] For example, see Nikaido ([18], Theorem 7.4, p. 107; [19], Theorem 20.2, p. 137).

$M(\pi) = 0$ is essentially not different from that in the preceding theorem, since Equation (VI.44) reduces to Equation (VI.13).

The situation $M(\pi) > 0$ will now be discussed. The basic idea in the method of proof remains to be the same as in the Say's case, but will be worked out in terms of a different mapping. Let the mapping $V : R^n_+ \rightarrow R^n$ be defined by

$$V(x) = x - \left\{ \left(A + \frac{F(p, 1)l'}{L(p, 1)} \right) x + G(p, \pi_1 x_1, \ldots, \pi_n x_n) \right\}.$$

(VI.61)

The Jacobian matrix $J_V(x)$ of the mapping is given by

$$J_V(x) = I - \left\{ A + \frac{F(p, 1)l'}{L(p, 1)} + \left(\frac{\partial G_i}{\partial s_j} \right) \begin{pmatrix} \pi_1 & & 0 \\ & \pi_2 & \\ & & \ddots \\ 0 & & \pi_n \end{pmatrix} \right\}$$

(VI.62)

similarly as in (VI.50). In the light of the price equation, again, the full spending of wage incomes and the less-than-one marginal propensities to spend of the capitalist households (VI.46), evaluation can readily be done, obtaining

$$p'J_V(x) \geq (1 - \epsilon)\pi' \geq 0.$$
(VI.63)

$M(\pi) > 0$ rules out $\pi = 0$, which ensures the semi-positivity of $(1 - \epsilon)\pi'$ in (VI.63).

From the basic assumptions including the indecomposability of A and the hypothesis of no inferior goods, it follows that the matrix in the braces in (VI.62) is an indecomposable nonnegative matrix. Therefore the truth of (VI.63) for the positive p implies by virtue of the Hawkins-Simon result [10] reinforced by indecomposability[22] that all

---

[22] For example, see Nikaido ([18], Theorem 7.4, p. 107; [19], Theorem 20.2, p. 137).

the principal minors of $J_V(x)$ are positive. From here on, the proof can proceed on the basis of the univalence theorems referred to in the course of the proof of the preceding theorem in essentially the same way to see that the mapping V is univalent on R^n_+, and that the inverse mapping V^{-1} : $V(R^n_+) \longrightarrow R^n_+$ is monotonic-increasing.

Now, Equation (VI.44) can be rearranged to

$$V(x) = \omega d. \tag{VI.64}$$

Suppose then that there are two distinct solutions $\{x^1, \omega^1\}$ and $\{x^2, \omega^2\}$. They satisfy (VI.64), so that

$$V(x^t) = \omega^t d \quad (t = 1, 2). \tag{VI.65}$$

One must have $\omega^1 \neq \omega^2$. For otherwise the univalence of V implies $x^1 = x^2$ in (VI.65), contradicting $\{x^1, \omega^1\} \neq \{x^2, \omega^2\}$. Without loss of generality it may therefore be assumed that

$$\omega^1 > \omega^2. \tag{VI.66}$$

Since d is assumed to be semi-positive, the monotonic increasingness of the inverse mapping V^{-1} and (VI.66) ensure

$$x^1 = V^{-1}(\omega^1 d) \geq V^{-1}(\omega^2 d) = x^2. \tag{VI.67}$$

With the above results in mind, let Equation (VI.44) be rearranged again to

$$x = (I - A)^{-1} \left\{ \frac{l'xF(p, 1)}{L(p, 1)} + \omega d + G(p, \pi_1 x_1, \dots, \pi_n x_n) \right\}. \tag{VI.68}$$

The matrix $(I - A)^{-1}$ is positive in (VI.68) by the indecomposability of A. Moreover, $l'x^1 > l'x^2$ in (VI.68) because (VI.67) and the positivity of l, so that

$$\frac{l'x^1 F(p, 1)}{L(p, 1)} \geq \frac{l'x^2 F(p, 1)}{L(p, 1)}. \tag{VI.69}$$

(VI.66) and $d \geq 0$ imply

$$\omega^1 d \geq \omega^2 d, \tag{VI.70}$$

whereas the hypothesis of no inferior goods and (VI.67) ensure

$$G(p, \pi_1 x_1^1, \ldots, \pi_n x_n^1) \geq G(p, \pi_1 x_1^2, \ldots, \pi_n x_n^2). \tag{VI.71}$$

Therefore, the positivity of $(I - A)^{-1}$, (VI.69), (VI.70), and (VI.71) altogether give rise to

$$x^1 > x^2 \tag{VI.72}$$

through (VI.68) for $x = x^1, x^2$. (VI.72) implies that one of x^1 and x^2 cannot lie on the economy's efficient frontier, contradicting (V.43). This completes the proof.   Q.E.D.

VI.4. Objective demand functions under capacity limits

The reconstruction of objective demand functions has already been worked out substantially in the three foregoing sections in Chapter VI. It is recalled that what the results in III.1, III.2, and III.3 mean for the construction of objective demand functions was explained in the immediately following section III.4. The three sections VI.1, VI.2, and VI.3 are in exactly the same relation to the reconstruction of objective demand functions under capacity limits as III.1, III.2, and III.3 to the construction of the functions without capacity limits.

In both the Say's and Keynesian cases, given the profit per unit output vector π, there are a unique gross output vector x and the corresponding final demand vector c, together with the scale of investment ω in the Keynesian case, such that x lies on the economy's efficient frontier in the price situation determined by π. Therefore these magnitudes can be thought of as functions of π, and

$$x_j(\pi) \quad (j = 1, 2, \ldots, n) \tag{VI.73}$$

are the objective gross demand functions of the jth sectors, respectively. From the continuity of all the relevant underlying functions such as F and G it is readily seen that the objective demand functions, including $c(\pi)$ and $\omega(\pi)$, are continuous on the set of all nonnegative π's.

When the supply of labor $L(p, 1)$ is fully employed at the price situation determined by π even within the capacity limits, the values of the reconstructed objective demand functions at π coincide with the corresponding values of the original objective demand functions without capacity limits. In particular, both functions coincide with each other when the profit per unit output π_i is sufficiently high at least in one sector. For $L(p, 1)$ tends to zero as at least one π_i grows indefinitely to infinity, as was remarked in the courses of proofs for Theorems 2 and 11. Then, the values of $x_j(\pi)$ become less in all the sectors than the capacity limits m_j if at least one π_i is sufficiently high. Only labor is binding in this price situation, so that there is full employment. Obviously, this phenomenon occurs relative to the current levels of capacity limits m_j. Therefore the phenomenon occurs even for low profits per unit output, if the current capacity limits are high enough to allow the full employment of labor to be achieved.

CHAPTER VII

Monopolistically Competitive Pricing Modes and the Objective Demand Functions, Continued

VII.1. Introduction

The objective demand functions have been constructed on the assumption that not only workers but also capitalists' households behave as price-takers. Nonetheless, the capitalists as entrepreneurs do behave more or less as price setters. The price system, which regulates the workers' supply of labor and demand for goods, is determined by the capitalists' price-setting behaviors and the interactions thereof subject to certain constraints, including the objective demand functions. A specific one of possible alternative modes of monopolistic competition singles out a point as a final market equilibrium on the objective demand schedules, along which the markets of all the goods are always cleared, whether or not a final monopolistically competitive equilibrium is already prevalent.

This basic general view in this work remains valid for the reconstructed objective demand functions in the presence of capacity limits. In Chapter IV, certain alternative modes of entrepreneurial behaviors in monopolistic competition were discussed and shown to lead to a monopolistically competitive equilibrium on the objective demand schedules without capacity limits. The modes are joint surplus value maximization, joint profit maximization, and the noncooperative profit maximization of the Cournot-Negishi type motivated through entrepreneurial perception of the demand for goods. This section will discuss a few more alternative modes of entrepreneurial behaviors in monopolistic competition with special regards to capacity limits, fixed equipment of production and machinery. Before proceeding to the main theme in this chapter, however, it will be noted that the three alternative modes discussed in Chapter IV can be applied *mutatis mutandis* to the situation where capacity limits are present.

First, not maximization of the potential surplus value but that of the utilized surplus value will be carried out, when capacity limits bind production. In this respect two alternative maximands are to be considered and distinguished from each other because of the presence of capacity limits. To discuss the Say's case, the maximand will be either

$$\sigma'c \qquad\qquad\qquad (VII.1)$$

or

$$\sigma'G(p, \pi_1 x_1(\pi), \pi_2 x_2(\pi), \ldots, \pi_n x_n(\pi)), \qquad (VII.2)$$

where σ = the labor value vector, c = the capitalists' final demand vector, and $x(\pi)$ = the objective gross demand function. One of the two alternative problems of surplus value maximization is to maximize (VII.1) by controlling c and π, and therefore also p through the price equation, subject to the constraints (VI.11). Needless to say, the capacity limits have already been incorporated into $x(\pi)$ in the other problem simply to maximize (VII.2) by controlling π and therefore also p through the price equation. A maximum can be shown to exist for each of both problems by a similar reasoning as that worked out in the proof of Theorem 2 in II.3.

However, it should be pointed out that the two problems lead in general to different solutions, which is a situation that never occurs in the absence of capacity limits. In the absence of capacity limits, the competitive choice of a final demand vector merely allocates the maximum surplus value among the n goods, once π is determined so as to maximize the surplus value as was noted earlier. The problem (VII.2) is a specific working-out of the problem (VII.1), and there is no discrepancy between them. But in the presence of capacity limits, the maximum surplus value of (VII.1) cannot always be achieved by maximizing (VII.2), since the solution of

(VII.2) may occur, due to the capacity limits, somewhere on the efficient frontier where the corresponding surplus value falls short of the maximum of (VII.1).

Second, no essential modification of the earlier reasoning in IV.2 is necessary to see that joint profit maximization can be achieved for the maximand $\pi'x(\pi)$, where $x(\pi)$ is the objective gross demand function under capacity limits.

Third, the formulation and discussion of the Cournot-Negishi solution in the absence of capacity limits in IV.3 work in their presence as well. It is reminded that the sectoral perceived demand functions are linear and downward sloping, except for the special case where they are horizontal, so that the optimal sectoral planned output levels occur as interior maxima of quadratic functions. This might cause a difficulty, since these optimal output levels are likely to be not within capacity limits. Nonetheless, they must coincide with the actual output levels given by the objective demand functions in the very equilibrium defined as a Cournot-Negishi solution. Therefore, if the formulation and discussion in IV.3 are worked out in terms of the objective demand functions under capacity limits, the existence of a Cournot-Negishi solution can be proved in the presence of capacity limits as well.

VII.2. Increasing returns and monopoly

It is an orthodox view in economic theory that monopoly is intimately related to increasing returns to scale. The basic model in this work is, however, the standard Leontief system in which constant returns to scale prevail, which might invite ᶜkepticism in the orthodox line. But here constant returns to scale prevail with regard to current input-output relations, and this fact by no means rules out increasing returns to scale in another context.

In this respect the basic view underlying this work is that increasing returns or decreasing costs phenomena occur with respect to the investment of fixed production equipment and machinery. A larger scale of their investment gives rise to a more-than-proportional increase in technological efficiency and capacity limits, causing increasing returns or decreasing costs. Notwithstanding, there are constant returns to scale with regard to the relation of current input of such variable factors as labor, raw material and semifinished goods to current output, once a plant is built, and production equipment and machinery are installed, while they bring about increasing returns.

These aspects of increasing returns to scale will be formulated in the following way. The production technology is reflected in the input coefficients a_{ij}, l_j and capacity limits m_j. These magnitudes may vary with the increase of the scales of fixed production equipment and machinery. Thus, the former can be regarded as functions of the latter.

The fixed equipment and machinery will be represented by a stock of the n goods.

$$K_{ij} \quad (i, j = 1, 2, \ldots, n), \tag{VII.3}$$

which may be called capital stock. More specifically, K_{ij} represents the amount of the ith good installed as capital stock in the jth sector. Then, a_{ij}'s, l_j's and m_j's are functions of K_{ij}'s. If there are neither economies nor diseconomies external to the sectors, these functions will be of the form

$$\begin{cases} a_{ij} = a_{ij}(K_{1j}, K_{2j}, \ldots, K_{nj}) \\ l_j = l_j(K_{1j}, K_{2j}, \ldots, K_{nj}) \\ m_j = m_j(K_{1j}, K_{2j}, \ldots, K_{nj}) \quad (i, j = 1, 2, \ldots, n). \end{cases} \tag{VII.4}$$

Naturally, a_{ij}'s and l_j's are decreasing functions, whereas m_j's are increasing functions. If there are indivisibilities, they are step-functions. Even if there are no indivisibilities and they are smooth, the capacity limit m_j is extremely tight for lower levels of capital stock K_{ij} in the jth sector because of increasing returns to scale. Figure 5 depicts the graph of the func-

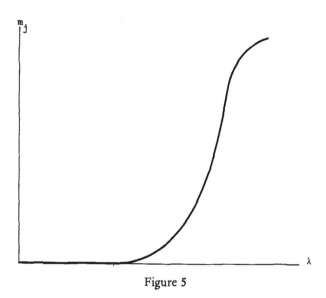

Figure 5

tion

$$m_j(\lambda) = m_j(\lambda K_{1j}, \lambda K_{2j}, \ldots, \lambda K_{nj}) \qquad \text{(VII.5)}$$

of the scale factor λ for a fixed set of levels of K_{ij}'s, and illustrates this aspect. A plausible shape of the graph of the function

$$a_{ij}(\lambda) = a_{ij}(\lambda K_{1j}, \lambda K_{2j}, \ldots, \lambda K_{nj}) \qquad \text{(VII.6)}$$

is also given in Figure 6. Figure 5 also illustrates decreasing returns to scale which might set in as λ becomes very large.

It may be plausible to presume that the functions m_j's in (VII.4) are superadditive, for certain ranges of the levels of capital stock where increasing returns prevail, in such a sense that

$$m_j(K_{1j}^1 + K_{1j}^2, \ldots, K_{nj}^1 + K_{nj}^2)$$
$$> m_j(K_{1j}^1, \ldots, K_{nj}^1) + m_j(K_{1j}^2, \ldots, K_{nj}^2). \qquad \text{(VII.7)}$$

111

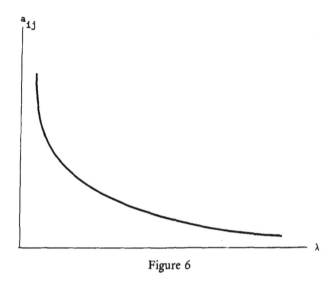

Figure 6

This shows that the jth sector consisting of a single firm equipped with the capital stock $K_{ij}^1 + K_{ij}^2$ $(i = 1, 2, \ldots, n)$ has larger capacities than that consisting of two firms equipped with K_{ij}^1 and K_{ij}^2 $(i = 1, 2, \ldots, n)$, respectively. Moreover, the giant firm can take advantage of smaller input coefficients than the latter two split firms, because of the decreasing property of $a_{ij}(K_{1j}, \ldots, K_{nj})$. Thus monopoly is very much likely to emerge.

VII.3. Entry-preventing price levels

Throughout this work, it has been presumed that each sector in the economy is a decision-making unit. This presumption has enabled me to envisage the bare socioeconomic aspects of the market price mechanism in the monopolistically competitive national economy without being vexed by complications that would arise from breaking down the sectors to individual firms. Therefore, the economy as a whole can be regarded as a huge market where there is complete product differentiation and each item is produced and supplied by a distinct monopolist, so that monopolistic competition prevails there in a similar, though not completely the same, sense as set forth in the orthodox economic theory (cf. Chamberlin [3]).

The above situation can be a reality, rather than a presumption. There might be severe competition among rival firms in each sector. But increasing returns could drive all the firms out from the sector but the fittest, as was remarked in VII.2.

The surviving monopolists can control market price formation, as was elucidated. Nevertheless, they may not charge arbitrarily high prices for their products, lest any potential entrant actually come in. Thus, there may be some entry-preventing price levels that keep any potential entrant driven out from the market.

Fortunately, much of the entry-preventing aspects of monopolistic pricing can be accounted for by the dual version of the so-called substitution theorem on Leontief systems established by Morishima ([13]; [14] Ch. IV, Theorem 1), if it is interpreted in a suitable context. The dual substitution theorem will be adapted as Theorem 20 below to the situation in question here, and its proof will be given, simply for easier reference.

Suppose that there are a finite number of potential firms $\tau_j \in T_j = \{1, 2, \ldots, t_j\}$ having input coefficients

$$a_{ij}(\tau_j), l_j(\tau_j) \quad (i = 1, 2, \ldots, n), \tag{VII.8}$$

respectively. Labor is aways indispensable, so that

$$l_j(\tau_j) > 0 \quad (\tau_j \in T_j). \tag{VII.9}$$

Let, further,

$$\pi_j(\tau_j) \geqq 0 \quad (\tau_j \in T_j) \tag{VII.10}$$

be the expected profit per unit output of the firm τ_j. It should be borne in mind that the input coefficients are given constant data, while the expected profits per unit output are variables.

Next, a cost function be defined for each sector j by

$$\rho_j(p, \pi_j(1), \ldots, \pi_j(t_j)) = \min_{\tau_j \in T_j} \left[\sum_{i=1}^{n} a_{ij}(\tau_j)p_i + l_j(\tau_j) + \pi_j(\tau_j) \right]$$
$$(j = 1, 2, \ldots, n) \qquad (\text{VII.11})$$

on the set of all nonnegative price vector $p = (p_i)$ and the set of all expected profits per unit output.

Theorem 20. *Assume that an input coefficient matrix* $A(*) = (a_{ij}(\tau_j^*))$ *which has the input coefficients of a firm* τ_j^* *from among* T_j *in its jth column* $(j = 1, 2, \ldots, n)$, *respectively, is viable enough to produce a positive final demand vector. Then, given any values of the expected profits per unit output of all the firms, the following facts hold true:*

(i) *The system of equations*

$$p_j = \rho_j(p, \pi_j(1), \ldots, \pi_j(t_j)) \quad (j = 1, 2, \ldots, n) \qquad (\text{VII.12})$$

has a unique positive price solution vector p^α.

(ii) $p^\alpha \leq p^\beta$ *for the price vector* p^β *determined by any viable input coefficients matrix* $A(\beta) = (a_{ij}(\tau_j^\beta))$, $\tau_j^\beta \in T_j$ $(j = 1, 2, \ldots, n)$, *through the system of equations*

$$p_j^\beta = \sum_{i=1}^{n} a_{ij}(\tau_j^\beta)p_i^\beta + l_j(\tau_j^\beta) + \pi_j(\tau_j^\beta) \quad (j = 1, 2, \ldots, n).$$

$$(\text{VII.13})$$

Proof. First, the existence of a solution will be proved. The viable input coefficients matrix $A(*)$ uniquely determines a positive price vector p^* through Equation (VII.13) for $\beta = *$. Let

$$\Delta = \{ p \mid p^* \geq p \geq 0 \}. \tag{VII.14}$$

For a price vector p in Δ one sees

$$\rho_j(p, \pi_j(1), \ldots, \pi_j(t_j)) \leq \sum_{i=1}^{n} a_{ij}(\tau_j^*) p_i + l_j(\tau_j^*) + \pi_j(\tau_j^*)$$

$$\leq \sum_{i=1}^{n} a_{ij}(\tau_j^*) p_i^* + l_j(\tau_j^*) + \pi_j(\tau_j^*) = p_j^*$$

$$(j = 1, 2, \ldots, n). \tag{VII.15}$$

In (VII.15), the first inequality is ensured by definition (VII.11), and the second inequality by $p^* \geq p$ and the non-negativity of the input coefficients, and finally the rightmost equality comes from the definition of p^*. If the continuous mapping $\rho : \Delta \longrightarrow R_+^n$ is defined by,

$$\rho(p) = (\rho_j(p, \pi_j(1), \ldots, \pi_j(t_j))), \tag{VII.16}$$

(VII.15) means that it maps the set Δ into itself. Δ is a cube, which is a compact convex set. Therefore the mapping has a fixed point $p^\alpha = \rho(p^\alpha)$ in Δ by virtue of the Brouwer fixed point theorem, and p^α is a desired solution.

The uniqueness of solution is an immediate consequence of proposition (ii). In fact, if a second solution p^β of (VII.12) occurs, it is characterized as a solution of (VII.13) for a specific β. Hence $p^\beta \geq p^\alpha$ by (ii). If the roles of p^α and p^β are interchanged, the same reasoning leads to $p^\alpha \geq p^\beta$. Thus, $p^\alpha = p^\beta$.

To prove (ii), let the row vectors $l'(\beta)$ and $\pi'(\beta)$ be defined by

$$l'(\beta) = (l_1(\tau_1^\beta), l_2(\tau_2^\beta), \ldots, l_n(\tau_n^\beta)) \tag{VII.17}$$

$$\pi'(\beta) = (\pi_1(\tau_1^\beta), \pi_2(\tau_2^\beta), \ldots, \pi_n(\tau_n^\beta)). \tag{VII.18}$$

Then

$$(p^\alpha)' = \rho(p^\alpha)' \le (p^\alpha)' A(\beta) + l'(\beta) + \pi'(\beta) \qquad \text{(VII.19)}$$

$$(p^\beta)' = (p^\beta)' A(\beta) + l'(\beta) + \pi'(\beta). \qquad \text{(VII.20)}$$

(VII.19) is implied by the definition of the mapping ρ, while (VII.20) is (VII.13) as expressed in a matrix form. Therefore subtraction of (VII.19) from (VII.20) gives

$$(p^\beta - p^\alpha)' (I - A(\beta)) \ge 0'. \qquad \text{(VII.21)}$$

$I - A(\beta)$ is invertible and has a nonnegative inverse because of the viability of $A(\beta)$. Finally, postmultiplication of (VII.21) by the nonnegative inverse matrix preserves the sense of inequality and gives rise to $p^\beta - p^\alpha \ge 0$, as was to be shown.

Q.E.D.

Once levels of all the potential firms' expected profits per unit output are set up, competition pushes prices down to p^α, the unique price system determined by Equation (VII.12). As is obvious from the meaning of Equation (VII.11), only some of the potential firms in each sector can realize their expected profits per unit output, while the other less competent firms could only achieve lower levels of their profits per unit output than they expected, or would incur losses if they entered or remained in the markets.

Now, from the definition of the functions ρ_j in (VII.11) it is evident that the price vector p^α determined by Equation (VII.12) is a function of the potential firms' expected profits per unit output (VII.10). It is also evident from the definition that this function is increasing with the expected profits per unit output. Therefore, the lowest p^α is reached when all the potential firms expect the profits per unit output to be zero, their lowest nonnegative levels. The corresponding lowest price vector p^α is the system's labor value vector, which could be identified as σ. Thus, the labor value vector σ could be thought of as the unique solution vector of a special case of Equation (VII.12), that is,

$$p_j = \rho_j(p, 0, 0, \ldots, 0) \quad (j = 1, 2, \ldots, n). \qquad \text{(VII.22)}$$

At $p^\alpha = \sigma$ only some of the potential firms can realize their expected zero profits per unit output, while all the other incompetent potential firms must be prepared to incur losses if they ever intend to enter the markets. Generally, there may still be more than one competent firm in each sector. However, it is also a conceivable situation that the minimum cost is achieved by a single firm τ_j^α in each sector j in Equation (VII.11) for $p = \sigma$. Then

$$\sigma_j = \sum_{i=1}^{n} a_{ij}(\tau_j^\alpha)\sigma_i + l_j(\tau_j^\alpha) < \sum_{i=1}^{n} a_{ij}(\tau_j)\sigma_i + l_j(\tau_j)$$

$$(\tau_j \in T_j,\, \tau_j \neq \tau_j^\alpha \,; j = 1, 2, \ldots, n). \qquad \text{(VII.23)}$$

Now, suppose that the competent firm in each sector expects its profit per unit output to be

$$\pi_j(\tau_j^\alpha) \geqq 0 \quad (j = 1, 2, \ldots, n). \qquad \text{(VII.24)}$$

Specification of the levels of $\pi_j(\tau_j^\alpha)$ in (VII.24) determines the corresponding prices p_j^α through Equation (VII.13) for $\beta = \alpha$. If these specified levels are low enough, continuity ensures, by virtue of (VII.23), the inequalities

$$p_j^\alpha = \sum_{i=1}^{n} a_{ij}(\tau_j^\alpha)p_i^\alpha + l_j(\tau_j^\alpha) + \pi_j(\tau_j^\alpha) < \sum_{i=1}^{n} a_{ij}(\tau_j)p_i^\alpha + l_j(\tau_j)$$

$$(\tau_j \in T_j,\, \tau_j \neq \tau_j^\alpha \,; j = 1, 2, \ldots, n). \qquad \text{(VII.25)}$$

In (VII.25) the firm τ_j^α can earn a positive level of the profit per unit output, but all the other firms in the jth sector would incur losses, if they ever intend to enter the market. Thus the firm τ_j^α can monopolize the supply of the jth good, while keeping all the other potential firms in the sector driven out from the market of the jth good, whenever the monopolists' expected profits per unit output are low enough to let (VII.25) hold.

Using (VII.17), (VII.18), and (VII.20) for $\beta = \alpha$, one has

$$(p^\alpha)' = \sigma' + \pi'(\alpha) \, (I - A(\alpha))^{-1} \qquad (\text{VII.26})$$

where

$$\sigma' = l'(\alpha) \, (I - A(\alpha))^{-1} \qquad (\text{VII.27})$$

Then, one can get a system of linear inequalities of unknowns $\pi_j(\tau_j^\alpha)$ $(j = 1, 2, \ldots, n)$ by substituting (VII.26) for p_j^α in (VII.25). This system of linear inequalities gives the exact range of such $\pi_j(\tau_j^\alpha)$'s as secure the monopolist position for the firm τ_j^α $(j = 1, 2, \ldots, n)$. It should also be noted that the interindustry ties, peculiar to the Leontief system, require all the monopolists in the entire economy to be modest in charging their profit margins in order to secure the monopolist position even for a single monopolist among them.

The input coefficients a_{ij}'s and l_j's of the economy could be identified to be the above $a_{ij}(\tau_j^\alpha)$'s and $l_j(\tau_j^\alpha)$'s. The technological superiority of $a_{ij}(\tau_j^\alpha)$'s and $l_j(\tau_j^\alpha)$'s over the input coefficients of the other potential firms may be based on the increasing-returns effect of their large capital stocks such as represented by (VII.4). Moreover, the technological discrepancy between the competent and incompetent firms could further be widened by the possibility that the functions (VII.4) available to the competent firms are superior to those available to the incompetent ones.

If the monopolists are seriously anxious about possible entrants, they will not dare to charge higher prices for their products than the entry-preventing ones by demanding profit margins that exceed the above range. Then the maximization of surplus value or joint profit will be carried out within that range, rather than on all possible profit margins. Nevertheless, if the right-hand sides are exceedingly larger in (VII.23) than the corresponding left-hand sides, the entry-preventing levels of prices can possibly be high enough to allow the unconstrained maximum of surplus value or joint profit already to occur within the range. Moreover, the perception of the monopolists who are anxious about entry may reflect their anxiety in such a way that their inverse perceived demand functions never take on entry-stimulating levels of prices. Therefore, the Cournot-Negishi solution turns out to be within the entry-preventing prices.

VII.4. Equal rates of returns

So far, no mention has been made of the ownerships of the capitalists in the economy, and they seem to have been, as it were, capitalists who own no capital. Now it is time to touch on their ownerships.

It may be a plausible presumption that the capital stock K_{ij} $(i, j = 1, 2, \ldots, n)$, which are installed in the sectors, respectively, and underlie their input coefficients and capacity limits, are owned by capitalists. It is, however, more plausible to presume that they own money capital to invest on the circulating capital as well as the fixed capital.

Now, suppose that they are concerned with rates of returns to the invested money capital, rather than surplus value, the absolute levels of profit or any other target magnitudes. If the voices of the sectors are equally powerful and influential, a possible alternative pricing mode in monopolistic competition will be the achievement of equal sectoral rates of returns to the invested money capital.

The purpose of this section is to formulate such a state of equal rates of returns and to prove its existence within the entry-preventing levels of prices.

If the profits per unit output π_j are specified in some way or another, this specification determines the prices p_j through the price equations, as was frequently remarked. The π_j's and p_j's further determine the levels of the objective gross demand functions $x_j(\pi)$. Then, the jth sector's rate of returns to the invested money capital is given by

$$r_j(\pi) = \frac{\pi_j x_j(\pi)}{x_j(\pi)\left(\sum_{i=1}^{n} a_{ij} p_i + l_j\right) + \sum_{i=1}^{n} K_{ij} p_i} \qquad (j = 1, 2, \ldots, n),$$

(VII.28)

where K_{ij}'s are nonnegative, and most likely positive.

Here, it is typical of the capital stocks that their monetary values function as fixed overhead costs, as contrasted to such variable costs items as wages, raw material and semifinished goods. Consequently, decreasing average costs prevail.

Now, a state of equal rates of returns to the invested money capital is characterized by

$$r_1(\pi) = r_2(\pi) = \ldots = r_n(\pi), \qquad (VII.29)$$

and achieved when the profits per unit output π_j are at some appropriate levels, as will be ensured by the following theorem.

Theorem 21. *There is a state of equal positive rates of returns to the invested money capital for some appropriate levels of the profits per unit output and the corresponding prices thereby determined. Moreover, this is still possible within the entry-preventing barrier.*

Proof. It is reminded that assumption [A.5] set forth in II.1 says that the labor force is willing to work at the special price situation $\pi = 0$, $p = \sigma$ and $w = 1$, so that $L(\sigma, 1) > 0$. Needless to say, the potential surplus value $M(0)$ is zero in this situation. If the indecomposability of the input coefficients matrix A is explicitly taken into account, the value of the objective gross demand function under capacity limits is a positive vector

$$x(0) > 0, \qquad (VII.30)$$

since it is a vector on the economy's efficient frontier which satisfies Equation (VI.13). Then continuity ensures

$$x(\pi) > 0, \qquad\qquad\qquad (VII.31)$$

when the profits per unit output π_j are low enough to keep the value of $x(\pi)$ close to $x(0)$.

Let ϵ be a positive number, and denote by S_ϵ the set of all profit per unit output vectors π whose components π_j add up to ϵ, obtaining

$$\sum_{j=1}^{n} \pi_j = \epsilon. \qquad\qquad\qquad (VII.32)$$

If ϵ is sufficiently small, (VII.31) holds for any π in S_ϵ, so that one can define the average cost functions

$$\omega_j(\pi) = \sum_{i=1}^{n} a_{ij}p_i + l_j + \frac{1}{x_j(\pi)}\sum_{i=1}^{n} K_{ij}p_i \quad (j = 1, 2, \ldots, n)$$

$$(VII.33)$$

for $\pi \in S_\epsilon$. Here, needless to say, p is determined by π through the price equation.

Next, define the continuous mapping $\mu : S_\epsilon \longrightarrow S_\epsilon$ by

$$\begin{cases} \mu(\pi) = (\mu_j(\pi)) \\ \\ \mu_j(\pi) = \dfrac{\epsilon\omega_j(\pi)}{\displaystyle\sum_{k=1}^{n} \omega_k(\pi)} \quad (j = 1, 2, \ldots, n). \end{cases} \qquad (VII.34)$$

The construction of the mapping can be worked out, since the average cost functions are positive-valued. Then, there is a fixed point $\hat{\pi}$ of the mapping in the simplex by virtue of the Brouwer fixed point theorem. Therefore $\hat{\pi} = \mu(\hat{\pi})$, which implies

$$r_1(\hat{\pi}) = r_2(\hat{\pi}) = \ldots = r_n(\hat{\pi}) = \frac{\epsilon}{\displaystyle\sum_{k=1}^{n} \omega_k(\hat{\pi})}, \qquad \text{(VII.35)}$$

as was to be shown. Moreover, S_ϵ can also be included in the entry-preventing range by making ϵ smaller, if necessary, and the above state is possible even within the entry-preventing barrier. Q.E.D.

A review of the proof of Theorem 21 will lead to the following information. For a given positive ϵ, the method of proof can be worked out, if $x(\pi)$ remains to be positive on the corresponding simplex S_ϵ, so that there is a state of equal rates of returns. This is the case, whenever the supply of labor $L(p, 1)$ remains to be positive on S_ϵ. On the other hand, if $L(p, 1) = 0$ for some π in S_ϵ, the corresponding value of the objective gross demand function $x(\pi)$ must be zero. In such a situation all the nominators in (VII.28) vanish, and the rates of returns are zero throughout the economy, which is a state of equal rates of returns. Finally, if $\epsilon = 0$, S_ϵ consists of a single element $\pi = 0$, for which there is also a state of equal zero rates of returns. In summary, there is a state of equal rates of returns for any given nonnegative value of ϵ.

From the above remark and the continuity of the relevant functions it follows that the set of all π's ensuring a state of equal rates of returns is an unbounded closed subset of the totality of all possible profit per unit output vectors. Its intersection with the entry-preventing range of π's, determined by the system of linear inequalities (VII.25), including its boundary facets, is therefore a compact set. On the other hand, the rates of returns are continuous functions of π, and they coincide with each other on the compact set. Hence there is such a state of equal rates of returns that its corresponding rate of returns is a maximum on the compact set.

This maximum must be positive from Theorem 21. If the maximum occurs off the entry-preventing barrier, this will be a plausible state of monopolistically competitive equilibrium. If the maximum occurs on the barrier, the equal rates of returns will never reach a maximum but can be indefinitely increased within the barrier. Nonetheless, the equal rates of returns are bounded not only within the barrier but also on the entire unbounded set of π's ensuring a state of equal rates of returns for the following reason. In fact, if (VII.29) holds with the common rate of returns r, one has

$$p_j = (1 + r) \left(\sum_{i=1}^{n} a_{ij} p_i + l_j \right) + \frac{r}{x_j(\pi)} \sum_{i=1}^{n} K_{ij} p_i$$

$$(j = 1, 2, \ldots, n). \quad \text{(VII.36)}$$

From (VII.36) it is clear that the matrix $I - (1 + r)A$ must be invertible and have a nonnegative inverse. This implies

$$\frac{1}{1 + r} > \lambda(A), \quad \text{(VII.37)}$$

where $\lambda(A)$ is the dominant nonnegative eigenvalue of A, the Frobenius root, and r is bounded, if $\lambda(A)$ is positive.[23]

[23] $\lambda(A) = 0$ is equivalent to $A^n = 0$, $n = $ order of A. Hence, in particular, $\lambda(A)$ is positive, when A is indecomposable.

CHAPTER VIII

Welfare Aspects of the Price Mechanism, Continued

VIII.1. Resource allocations under capacity limits

As has been brought to light in Chapter V, the allocation of labor and distribution of product among workers and capitalists implemented by the price mechanism achieve a Pareto optimum in the absence of capacity limits, if and only if the prices of goods coincide with their labor values and there is no surplus value, or equivalently, there are no profit incomes. In the absence of capacity limits, the only owners of factors that bind production are workers who own themselves as human capital, while capitalists own no binding factors. This situation specifies the competitive equilibrium to a situation of no surplus value as the only possible Pareto efficient state attained via the price mechanism. Any other resource allocation implemented by the price mechanism invalidates Pareto efficiency, and its normative implication can be assessed in comparison with the competitive equilibrium corresponding to the specific endowment and private ownership of factors of production.

What will happen in the presence of capacity limits? In this alternative situation, capitalists show up as capitalists, that is, as owners of capital stock underlying the capacity limits, so that there is an alternative state of endowment and private ownership of factors of production. This may result in an alternative specification of competitive equilibrium as a normatively meaningful state of resource allocation in comparison with which any other resource allocation implemented by the price mechanism can be evaluated. Now, the question to examine is whether a competitive equilibrium exists and can be characterized as the only possible Pareto

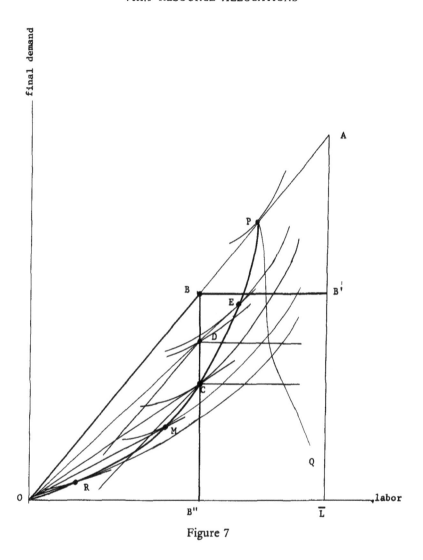

Figure 7

optimum implemented by the price mechanism under capacity limits. The examination will be carried out in the present chapter.

The examination starts with a diagrammatic reconsideration of the one good-one worker-one capitalist situation taken up in Section V.3. Suppose that there is a positive capacity

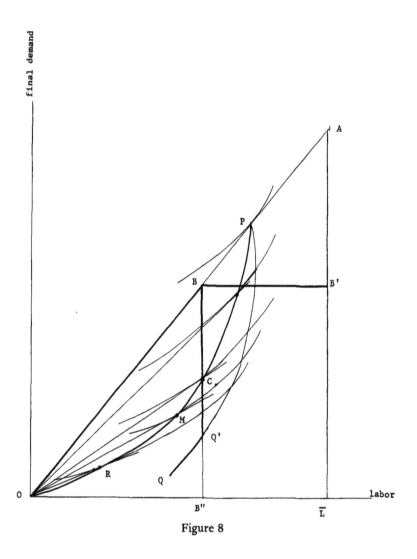

Figure 8

limit of gross output binding the final demand producible c within the domain $\bar{c} \geq c \geq 0$. The final demand is not producible beyond the limit $\bar{c}$, whatever amount of labor service may be further employed. If $\bar{c}$ actually limits the production possibility, the society's transformation curve degenerates from the linear segment OA in Figure 4 to the kinked segment OBB′ in Figures 7 and 8. In both figures the corresponding box diagrams are the trapezoid OBB'$\overline{L}$, where the worker's share in the final demand is measured in the positive direction of the vertical axis starting on the horizontal axis, but that of the capitalist is measured in the negative direction of the vertical axis starting on the kinked line OBB'. The worker's indifference curves are upward sloping curves as before, whereas those of the capitalist are kinked lines parallel to OBB', with their kinks lying on the vertical segment BB''.

In this new situation, the contract curve, that is, the set of Pareto optima may be differently shaped, depending on the location of the contract curve in the absence of capacity limits PQ relative to segment BB''. In Figure 7 PQ lies entirely to the right of BB'', and the new contract curve coincides with BB''. In Figure 8, PQ lies partly to the right and to the left of BB'', and the corresponding contract curve is BQ'Q. The reader may conceive an alternative situation where a more intricate position of PQ relative to BB'' results in complication in the structure of the contract curve.

It is now clear from topological intuition that the worker's offer curve intersects the contract curve somewhere, say, at C. In the price situation corresponding to the straight line OC, the capitalist is maximizing his profit as a price-taking entrepreneur subject to the transformation curve OBB' at C. He employs OB'' units of labor service to get the total net output BB'', of which he pays out B''C as wage bill and earns the profit BC. On the other hand the worker supplies OB'' units of labor service and demands for B''C to maximize his utility subject to the budget constraint. There is no need for the capitalist to allocate his profit income to several goods in the one-good world. Thus, C represents a competitive equilibrium.

It is also clear from topological intuition that competitive equilibrium need not be unique, as the worker's offer curve may or may not intersect the contract curve more than once. However, it must occur on the segment BB'', if P does not belong to the contract curve. For PQ and the offer curve have only one point P in common, as was noted in Section V.3.

A competitive equilibrium is a Pareto optimum implemented by the price mechanism. There are, however, Pareto optima which are implemented by the price mechanism without being competitive equilibria. It is recalled that the objective demand functions have been reconstructed under capacity limits in Chapter VI. Labor is underemployed if too much labor is supplied relative to the capacity limits in a price situation. In the price situation corresponding to the line OE, full employment is impossible, so that only OB″ units of labor are employed to produce BB″ units of final demand within the capacity limit. The worker's share in the final demand is B″D and that of the capitalist is BD. Clearly D represents a Pareto optimum. The capitalist is maximizing his profit at D as a price-taker. But the worker's utility is not a maximum at D subject to the budget constraint. This pricing leads to a Pareto optimum, but does not ensure a competitive equilibrium. Incidentally, as is well-known in welfare economics, D can be a competitive equilibrium, if the good is differently priced and part of the profit income is transferred from the capitalist to the worker.

In spite of possible multiple competitive equilibria and Pareto optima implemented by the price mechanism, there is a point which is attainable by the price mechanism and located lowest on BB″. This point represents a competitive equilibrium, and both its corresponding good price and profit per unit output are the highest among those of Pareto optima achievable by the price mechanism. A higher profit per unit output than this competitive level must invalidate Pareto efficiency, and the amount by which the former exceeds the latter may be thought of as an excess profit per unit output. There is also unavoidable excess capacity in such a situation.

VIII.2. Competitive equilibrium under capacity limits

This and the following sections will see to what extent the foregoing diagrammatic analysis can be carried over to the general situation. The economy is now assumed to include

r workers $\alpha = 1, 2, \ldots, r$ and s capitalists' households $\beta = 1, 2, \ldots, s$, endowed with utility functions of the neo-classical type, respectively, as was formulated in Section V.1. This assumption means, in particular, that the corresponding aggregate demand function of the capitalist class $G(p, s_1, s_2, \ldots, s_n)$ is of the J. B. Say type.

On the objective demand schedule $x(\pi)$ in the absence of capacity limits, all the workers' and capitalists' households are maximizing their utilities subject to the budget constraints, and demand equals supply for every good, including the full employment of labor. Thus the only possible source of non-competitive working of the economy stems from the pricing modes of the capitalists as entrepreneurs. Therefore, a point on the objective demand schedule represents a competitive equilibrium if and only if the output is maximizing the profit in each sector under the price system taken as a parameter.

Let m_j be the capacity limit of the jth sector, as before, which is positive. If π_j is the jth sector's profit per unit output, the competitive equilibrium under the capacity limits $m = (m_j)$ is characterized as such a state that

$$m_j \geqq x_j(\pi) \quad (j = 1, 2, \ldots, n) \tag{VIII.1}$$

with equality holding if $\pi_j > 0$,

that is, the jth sector is maximizing the profit $\pi_j y_j$ at $y_j = x_j(\pi)$ subject to $m_j \geqq y_j \geqq 0$ for π_j taken as a given parameter. A competitive equilibrium is a special case of the Cournot-Negishi solution. In spite of the remark in Section VII.1, however, it is excluded from formula (IV.25) in the presence of capacity limits, and its existence needs a separate proof.

Theorem 22. *There is a competitive equilibrium, if the indecomposability of the input coefficients matrix A is explicitly assumed.*

Proof. Consider the continuous mapping $\Delta : R_+^n \longrightarrow R_+^n$,

where

$$\Delta(\pi) = (\delta_j(\pi)) \tag{VIII.2}$$

$$\delta_j(\pi) = \max(\pi_j + x_j(\pi) - m_j, 0) \quad (j = 1, 2, \ldots, n). \tag{VIII.3}$$

The basic price equation can be put in the form

$$p_j = \sigma_j + \sum_{i=1}^{n} b_{ij}\pi_i \quad (j = 1, 2, \ldots, n), \tag{VIII.4}$$

where $(b_{ij}) = (I - A)^{-1}$, which is a positive matrix by inde-composability. If $\epsilon = \min b_{ij}$ for all i, j, (VIII.4) implies that

$$p_j \geqq \sigma_j + \epsilon\eta \quad (j = 1, 2, \ldots, n) \tag{VIII.5}$$

for

$$\sum_{i=1}^{n} \pi_i \geqq \eta. \tag{VIII.6}$$

Hence, $p_j (j = 1, 2, \ldots, n)$ are very large if η is sufficiently large, so that $L(p, 1)$ is very small by virtue of assumption [A.4] given in Section II.1. Since the objective demand function satisfies nonnegativity and the identity

$$\sum_{j=1}^{n} l_j x_j(\pi) = L(p, 1),$$

this implies

$$x_j(\pi) < m_j \quad (j = 1, 2, \ldots, n) \tag{VIII.7}$$

for π fulfilling (VIII.6) if η is sufficiently large.

Now take η large enough to ensure (VIII.7). Then,

$$\sum_{j=1}^{n} \delta_j(\pi) < \sum_{j=1}^{n} \pi_j \qquad\qquad \text{(VIII.8)}$$

for π fulfilling (VIII.6). In fact,

$$0 = \delta_j(\pi) \leqq \pi_j$$

for j with the vanishing $\delta_j(\pi)$, and, in view of (VIII.7),

$$\delta_j(\pi) = \pi_j + x_j(\pi) - m_j < \pi_j$$

for j with the positive $\delta_j(\pi)$, whenever (VIII.6) holds. Then summation over all j leads to (VIII.8), if at least one $\delta_j(\pi)$ is positive. Otherwise, (VIII.8) also holds because of (VIII.6), $\eta > 0$.

The set of all $\pi \geq 0$ fulfilling

$$\sum_{j=1}^{n} \pi_j \leqq \eta \qquad\qquad \text{(VIII.9)}$$

is compact, and its image under the mapping Δ is bounded. Choose a simplex

$$\Omega = \left\{ \pi \mid \pi \geq 0, \sum_{j=1}^{n} \pi_j \leqq \rho \right\}$$

large enough to include the image.

Now let $\pi \in \Omega$. If π satisfies (VIII.9), the method of choosing Ω directly ensures $\Delta(\pi) \in \Omega$. If π does not, (VIII.8) ensures $\Delta(\pi) \in \Omega$. Hence, the mapping can be contracted to a continuous mapping $\Delta : \Omega \longrightarrow \Omega$. Consequently, there exists a fixed point π^c under Δ by virtue of the Brouwer fixed point theorem, so that

$$\pi_j^c = \max{(\pi_j^c + x_j(\pi^c) - m_j, 0)} \quad (j = 1, 2, \ldots, n).$$

$$\text{(VIII.10)}$$

(VIII.10) means

$$\pi_j^c \geqq \pi_j^c + x_j(\pi^c) - m_j \quad (j = 1, 2, \ldots, n), \qquad \text{(VIII.11)}$$

with equality holding if $\pi_j^c > 0$,

which amounts to (VIII.1) for $\pi = \pi^c$. The economy is in a competitive equilibrium at π^c. Q.E.D.

VIII.3. Monopolistic competition and Pareto inefficiency

As is well known, a competitive equilibrium is a Pareto optimum. In the absence of capacity limits, the competitive equilibrium that necessitates zero profit incomes is the only Pareto optimum that can be implemented by the price mechanism. The situation is somewhat different if there are capacity limits. Under the circumstances an underemployment equilibrium on the objective demand schedule, too, can be a Pareto optimum. This new situation calls for the characterization of Pareto optima implemented by the price mechanism.

Before proceeding to the characterization, it is necessary to have clearly in mind what a resource allocation implemented by the price mechanism is. Let

$$F^\alpha(p, 1), L^\alpha(p, 1) \quad (\alpha = 1, 2, \ldots, r) \qquad \text{(VIII.12)}$$

be the αth worker's individual demand function for goods and supply function of labor, derived from utility maximization subject to the budget constraint. These functions add up to the aggregate demand and supply functions

$$F(p, 1) = \sum_{\alpha=1}^{r} F^\alpha(p, 1) \qquad \text{(VIII.13)}$$

$$L(p, 1) = \sum_{\alpha=1}^{r} L^{\alpha}(p, 1). \tag{VIII.14}$$

Let $x(\pi) = (x_j(\pi))$ be the objective demand function under capacity limits. The determinate sectoral incomes $\pi_j x_j(\pi)$ $(j = 1, 2, \ldots, n)$ are distributed in a definite way, e.g. in fixed proportions, exclusively among the s capitalists' households. The income of the βth capitalist's household therefore consists of its share in the sectoral incomes and can be thought of as a nonnegative continuous function $I_{\beta}(\pi)$ $(\beta = 1, 2, \ldots, s)$. Utility maximization subject to the budget constraint $p'g^{\beta} = I_{\beta}(\pi)$ leads to the individual demand function $G^{\beta}(p, I_{\beta}(\pi))$ of the βth capitalist's household. These s individual demand functions add up to the aggregate demand function, so that

$$G(p, \pi_1 x_1(\pi), \pi_2 x_2(\pi), \ldots, \pi_n x_n(\pi)) = \sum_{\beta=1}^{s} G^{\beta}(p, I_{\beta}(\pi)).$$

$$\tag{VIII.15}$$

An allocation implemented by the price mechanism is an allotment of a pair of a final demand vector f^{α} and labor service L^{α} to the αth worker $(\alpha = 1, 2, \ldots, r)$ and a final demand vector g^{β} to the βth capitalist's household $(\beta = 1, 2, \ldots, s)$ such that for a $\pi \geq 0$,

$$p'f^{\alpha} = L^{\alpha} \tag{VIII.16}$$

$$\sum_{\alpha=1}^{r} f^{\alpha} = \theta F(p, 1) \tag{VIII.17}$$

$$\sum_{\alpha=1}^{r} L^{\alpha} = \theta L(p, 1) \quad (\alpha = 1, 2, \ldots, r) \tag{VIII.18}$$

$$\theta = l'x(\pi)/L(p, 1) \tag{VIII.19}$$

$$g^\beta = G^\beta (p, I_\beta(\pi)) \quad (\beta = 1, 2, \ldots, s) \tag{VIII.20}$$

In characterizing the Pareto optimum implemented by the price mechanism in the following theorem, all the neoclassical assumptions on the individual taste, including smooth and strictly convex indifference surfaces, will be utilized.

Theorem 23. *Let* f^α, L^α, $g^\beta (\alpha = 1, 2, \ldots, r;\ \beta = 1, 2, \ldots, s)$ *be an allocation implemented by the price mechanism.*

(i) *If the allocation is a Pareto optimum, then (A), (B) and (C) hold.*

(A) *Each sector is maximizing its profit* $\pi_j y_j$ *at* $y_j = x_j(\pi)$ *subject to* $m_j \geq y_j \geq 0$ *under* π_j *taken as a given parameter. Moreover* $x_j(\pi) = m_j$ $(j = 1, 2, \ldots, n)$ *if* $\theta < 1$.

(B) *The marginal utilities of workers satisfy*

$$\frac{\partial}{\partial f_i^\alpha} U^\alpha (f^\alpha, L^\alpha) \bigg/ - \frac{\partial}{\partial L^\alpha} U^\alpha (f^\alpha, L^\alpha) = \lambda p_i$$

$$\begin{pmatrix} i = 1, 2, \ldots, n \\ \alpha = 1, 2, \ldots, r \end{pmatrix} \tag{VIII.21}$$

for a common scalar $\lambda \geq 1$.

(C) $\lambda > 1$ *in the case of* $1 > \theta$. *Otherwise* $f^\alpha = F^\alpha (p, 1)$, $L^\alpha = L^\alpha (p, 1)$ *and* $\lambda = 1$.

(ii) *If (A) and (B) hold, then the allocation is a Pareto optimum.*

Proof. (i) As is well known, a price system (q, w) consisting of a good price vector q and a wage rate w is associated to the Pareto optimum allocation in question such that

$U^\alpha (f, L)$ is maximized at $f = f^\alpha$, $L = L^\alpha$

subject to $q'f - wL \leq q'f^\alpha - wL^\alpha$ $(\alpha = 1, 2, \ldots, r)$,

$$\tag{VIII.22}$$

$U^\beta(g)$ is maximized at $g = g^\beta$

subject to $q'g \leq q'g^\beta$ $(\beta = 1, 2, \ldots, s)$ $\qquad$ (VIII.23)

$$\left(q_j - \sum_{i=1}^{n} a_{ij}q_i - wl_j \right) y_j \text{ is maximized at } y_j = x_j(\pi)$$

subject to $m_j \geq y_j \geq 0$. $\qquad$ (VIII.24)

The proof will be worked out by examining the relation of (q, w) to $(p, 1)$. First of all, it is obvious from (VIII.20) and (VIII.23) that

$q = \mu p$ for a scalar $\mu > 0$. $\qquad$ (VIII.25)

If the positive disutility of labor is explicitly assumed, (VIII.22) and (VIII.25) imply (VIII.21) for

$$\lambda = \frac{\mu}{w},$$ $\qquad$ (VIII.26)

for which $\lambda \geq 1$ will be seen by proving (C).

To prove (C) it is noted that (VIII.16) means that f^α and L^α satisfy the budget constraint under the price situation $(p, 1)$, while the αth worker's taste singles out the unique optimum $F^\alpha(p, 1)$ and $L^\alpha(p, 1)$ subject to the same budget constraint. Hence

$$U^\alpha(F^\alpha(p, 1), L^\alpha(p, 1)) \geq U^\alpha(f^\alpha, L^\alpha) \quad (\alpha = 1, 2, \ldots, r).$$
$$\text{(VIII.27)}$$

If $\theta < 1$, it is impossible for all (f^α, L^α) to coincide with $(F^\alpha(p, 1), L^\alpha(p, 1))$, so that strict inequality holds for at least one relation in (VIII.27). In the light of (VIII.22) this implies

$$q'F^\alpha(p, 1) - wL^\alpha(p, 1) \geq q'f^\alpha - wL^\alpha \quad (\alpha = 1, 2, \ldots, r)$$
$$\text{(VIII.28)}$$

with strict inequality holding for at least one α.

Summing up (VIII.28) and using (VIII.13), (VIII.14), (VIII.17), (VIII.18), (VIII.25) and the basic relation $p'F(p, 1) = L(p, 1)$, one has

$$(1 - \theta)(\mu - w)L(p, 1) > 0, \qquad (\text{VIII.29})$$

which leads to

$$\mu > w \qquad (\text{VIII.30})$$

and

$$\lambda > 1$$

in (VIII.26).

Next consider the case $\theta = 1$. Then the Pareto optimality of the allocation rules out strict inequality in (VIII.27), and the strictly convex preference of each worker ensures $f^\alpha = F^\alpha(p, 1)$ and $L^\alpha = L^\alpha(p, 1)$ together with $\lambda = 1$ in (VIII.26). It remains to prove (A). By (VIII.25) one gets

$$q_j - \sum_{i=1}^{n} a_{ij}q_i - wl_j = \mu \pi_j + (\mu - w)l_j \quad (j = 1, 2, \ldots, n),$$

$$(\text{VIII.31})$$

where $\mu \geq w$ from the results already established. Then, if $\pi_j > 0$, the left-hand side of the jth relation in (VIII.31) is also positive, and one must have

$$x_j(\pi) = m_j \qquad (\text{VIII.32})$$

by (VIII.24), proving (A). Moreover, one has (VIII.30) if $\theta < 1$, as was shown above. In this case the left-hand side of (VIII.31) is positive for all $j = 1, 2, \ldots, n$. Whence (VIII.32) holds for all $j = 1, 2, \ldots, n$ by (VIII.24).

(ii) First consider the case $\theta = 1$. One has (VIII.27), which is ensured only by the definition of (VIII.12) and the fulfillment of the budget constraint (VIII.16), as in (i).

(VIII.21) implies that f^α and L^α are maximizing U^α (f, L) subject to $\lambda p' f - L \leq \lambda p' f^\alpha - L^\alpha$ $(\alpha = 1, 2, \ldots, r)$. From this and (VIII.27) it follows that

$$\lambda p' F^\alpha (p, 1) - L^\alpha (p, 1) \geq \lambda p' f^\alpha - L^\alpha \quad (\alpha = 1, 2, \ldots, r).$$

$$\text{(VIII.33)}$$

If there is at least one strict inequality in (VIII.27), strict inequality also holds for the corresponding relation in (VIII.33). Then, summation over all α in (VIII.33) leads to

$$\lambda p' F(p, 1) - L(p, 1) > \lambda p' F(p, 1) - L(p, 1)$$

by (VIII.17), (VIII.18) and $\theta = 1$, yielding a contradiction. Hence equality holds for all α in (VIII.27), and the strict convexity of preference ensures $f^\alpha = F^\alpha (p, 1)$ and $L^\alpha = L^\alpha (p, 1)$ for every worker. Therefore, (A) and (B) imply in this case $\theta = 1$ that the allocation is a competitive equilibrium and hence a Pareto optimum.

Next, suppose $\theta < 1$. Then the last part of (A) ensures (VIII.32), and the profit of each sector is maximized at $y_j = x_j (\pi)$ under the price system $(\lambda p, 1)$ taken as a parameter, with the corresponding profit per unit output being

$$\lambda p_j - \sum_{i=1}^{n} a_{ij} \lambda p_i - l_j = \lambda \pi_j + (\lambda - 1) l_j \quad (j = 1, 2, \ldots, n).$$

$$\text{(VIII.34)}$$

Now, if $(\lambda - 1) l' x (\pi)$ is transferred out of the profit income $\lambda \pi' x (\pi) + (\lambda - 1) l' x (\pi)$ to the workers, with the allotment to the αth worker being $t_\alpha = (\lambda - 1) L^\alpha$, the αth worker is maximizing his utility at $f = f^\alpha$ and $L = L^\alpha$ subject to the budget constraint $\lambda p' f - L \leq t_\alpha$ $(\alpha = 1, 2, \ldots, r)$ by (VIII.21) in (B). On the other hand, the capitalists' shares are $\lambda \pi_j x_j (\pi)$ by sector under the good price vector λp, so that their households demand for exactly the same bundles $G^\beta (\lambda p, I_\beta (\lambda \pi)) =$

$G^\beta(p, I_\beta(\pi))$ $(\beta = 1, 2, \ldots, s)$. Therefore the allocation is a Pareto optimum. This completes the proof. Q.E.D.

This theorem suggests the possibility of noncompetitive Pareto optimal allocations implemented by the price mechanism with involuntary unemployment. Nevertheless, it is also clear in the light of the theorem that excess capacity in a sector with positive profit indicates the Pareto inefficiency of the allocation implemented by the price mechanism. Likewise the coexistence of excess capacity in a sector and involuntary unemployment also indicates the same situation.

Provisional Epilogue

The present work is only a prelude to a general equilibrium theory of monopolistic competition from the notional point of view. Its primary purpose is to study how monopolists are mutually interdependent. The interdependence in question is not what the traditional oligopoly theorist has in mind in special regard to entrepreneurial behaviors, but the national economy-wide objective framework of interdependence to which the monopolists must be subjected. It binds the monopolists' potential behaviors, including their control of resource allocation and income distribution. It exists independently of the monopolists' perceptions and conjectures and embeds any possible monopolistically competitive equilibrium.

To recapitulate more specifically, this work stresses the source underlying the effective demand for the product of each monopolist, which can be determinate only simultaneously with the determination of all the sectoral output levels throughout the economy. This principle of effective demand leads to the construction of objective demand functions. Thus, the basic view in this work is that, in the monopoly capitalist economy peculiar to the present day, the balance of demand and supply is achieved through output adjustment, rather than price adjustment, while the latter is an instrument to regulate income distribution. The economy is thereby thought of as national economy-wide monopolistic competition among the monopoly sectors by means of pricing strategies within the framework represented by the objective demand functions.

In the monopolistic competition, pricing is worked out essentially, though not phenomenally, through the choice of sectoral profit levels per unit output. The mode of choice depends on the pattern of competition, with perfect competition and joint optimization as opposite extreme situations. Perfect competition is a situation in which sectoral profit levels per unit output are least controllable by the participants of the competition, and an invisible hand controls the choice. The more monopolistic the pattern becomes, the more controllable by the participants the profit levels become.

It is important to realize that the structural characteristics of the national economy-wide framework of monopolistic competition differ from what has been presumed in the traditional monopolistic competition theory and game theory. The objective demand function is not necessarily downward sloping, nor need the sectoral profit evaluated in terms of the function be concave. There are many pecuniary externalities. These difficulties call for the critical reexamination of the traditional solution concepts, which would work well in their absence.

The scope of this work is very limited. It is confined to the static notional aspects of national economy-wide monopolistic competition, with principal attention focused on the study of the structural framework of monopolists' control over national income distribution by means of pricing. Dynamic aspects such as investment and growth are not considered here and remain to be further studied.

Appendix

Oligopolistic Indeterminacy of Output Shares
and a Rationale for the Basic Presumption

Throughout this volume it is presumed that each sector behaves as a single decision-making unit. One rationale for the presumption is the domination of the sector by a technologically supreme firm through the establishment of entry-preventing price barriers, as was discussed in VII.3. For the sake of simplicity in analysis it is assumed there that a *single* firm τ_j^α dominates each sector, exclusively achieving the minimum cost in Equation (VII.11) for $p = \sigma$.

Nevertheless, there are likely to be several tying firms that can still survive when the prices equal the labor values determined by Equation (VII.22). Then an oligopolistic situation emerges in some sector. The firms can drive other incompetent firms out from the market by enforcing entry-preventing prices. Is a rationale still possible for the presumption in spite of a likely oligopolistic situation such that a number of competent firms remain in each sector? This appendix supplements the entire volume in this respect.

When several competent firms tie in each sector, the sectoral output levels are still determined in such a way that effective demand coming from spending of wages and profits equals supply for each good. But the determination of output levels is not unique in contrast with the unique determination ensured under the presumption in III.3 and VI.3, even if there are no inferior goods for capitalists' households. This is due to the oligopolistic indeterminacy of the competent firms' output shares in each sector. Notwithstanding the indeterminacy, if they, either tacitly or boldly, cooperate and agree upon *relative* shares of output, the sectoral output levels are uniquely determined. Furthermore, each sector can be presumed to consist of a single firm having a production technology of the Leontief type for the relative shares of output agreed upon. Thus, if the agreements among the competent firms on the relative shares of output are stable, we can be justified in assuming that each sector behaves as if it is a single decision-making unit.

The above remark can be made sure analytically in the following way. As was discussed in VII.3, the price vector p is uniquely determined by Equation (VII.12) once all potential firms $\tau_j \in T_j$ in each sector $j = 1, 2, \ldots, n$ specify their own expected nonnegative levels $\pi_j(\tau_j)$ of profit per unit output. Clearly, the minimum cost including the expected profit equals the corresponding price for some firms in T_j at this price vector p. Some other firms can still avoid a loss by being modest enough to reduce their initially expected levels of profit per unit output to new, lower, nonnegative levels. But yet another group of incompetent firms must incur losses in this price situation, so that their modified levels of expected unit profit can be only negative.

The group of firms last mentioned is driven out from the markets, while the first two groups of competent firms survive. Let $T_j(p)$ be the set of all these competent firms in the jth sector and $\pi_j(\tau_j)$, $\tau_j \in T_j(p)$ be the nonnegative expected levels of profit per unit output that exactly equate the cost including the expected profit to the price, respectively. Then

$$p_j = \sum_{i=1}^{n^\cdot} a_{ij}(\tau_j) p_i + l_j(\tau_j) + \pi_j(\tau_j) \quad \begin{pmatrix} \tau_j \in T_j(p) \\ j = 1, 2, \ldots, n \end{pmatrix}.$$

(A.1)

Suppose that a set of relative shares of output

$$\theta_j(\tau_j) \geqq 0, \quad \sum_{\tau_j \in T_j(p)} \theta_j(\tau_j) = 1$$

$$(\tau_j \in T_j(p), j = 1, 2, \ldots, n) \quad \text{(A.2)}$$

is arbitrarily prescribed and fixed. Then, first, in the price side, the linearity of (A.1) implies

$$p_j = \sum_{i=1}^{n} a_{ij} p_i + l_j + \pi_j \quad (j = 1, 2, \ldots, n) \tag{A.3}$$

for the same price vector p, where

$$a_{ij} = \sum_{\tau_j \in T_j(p)} a_{ij}(\tau_j) \theta_j(\tau_j) \tag{A.4}$$

$$l_j = \sum_{\tau_j \in T_j(p)} l_j(\tau_j) \theta_j(\tau_j) \tag{A.5}$$

$$\pi_j = \sum_{\tau_j \in T_j(p)} \pi_j(\tau_j) \theta_j(\tau_j) \quad (j = 1, 2, \ldots, n). \tag{A.6}$$

Second, in the output side, if supply equals effective demand originating from wages and profits without capacity limits in the Say's case, the total output vector $x = (x_j)$ must satisfy

$$\dot{x}_i = \sum_{j=1}^{n} \sum_{\tau_j \in T_j(p)} a_{ij}(\tau_j) \theta_j(\tau_j) x_j + F_i(p, 1)$$

$$+ G_i(p, s_1, s_2, \ldots, s_n) \quad (i = 1, 2, \ldots, n) \tag{A.7}$$

$$s_j = \sum_{\tau_j \in T_j(p)} \pi_j(\tau_j) \theta_j(\tau_j) x_j \quad (j = 1, 2, \ldots, n) \tag{A.8}$$

$$\sum_{j=1}^{n} \sum_{\tau_j \in T_j(p)} l_j(\tau_j) \theta_j(\tau_j) x_j = L(p, 1). \tag{A.9}$$

However, (A.7), (A.8), (A.9) can be aggregated with the weights (A.2) to

$$x_i = \sum_{j=1}^{n} a_{ij} x_j + F_i(p, 1) + G_i(p, \pi_1 x_1, \pi_2 x_2, \ldots, \pi_n x_n)$$

$$(i = 1, 2, \ldots, n) \qquad \text{(A.10)}$$

$$\sum_{j=1}^{n} l_j x_j = L(p, 1). \qquad \text{(A.11)}$$

(A.3), (A.10), with (A.11) are just the systems analyzed throughout the entire volume. Therefore, the unique determination of output levels under the given unit profit levels is ensured by virtue of the results already established.

If $p = \sigma$, the economy's labor value vector determined by Equation (VII.22), $T_j(\sigma)$ generally includes several competent firms, and $T_j(p)$ remains unchanged and equals $T_j(\sigma)$, when $\pi_j(\tau_j)$ for $\tau_j \in T_j(\sigma)$ are positive and *well-proportioned* but small enough to lie within the entry-preventing barriers. Undoubtedly the above remark can apply to the Keynesian case, too.

This justification of the basic presumption premises the determination of relative output shares through an agreement among competent firms in each sector, as is most likely to be the case, or else in some other way, e.g., through capacity limits. In general, however, it must be admitted that the relative shares are indeterminate, since arbitrary prescription of them is completely consistent with the working of the economy.

References

[1] Arrow, K. J., The Firm in General Equilibrium Theory, R. Marris and A. Wood, eds., *The Corporate Economy: Growth, Competition, and Innovative Potential*, Harvard University Press, Cambridge, Massachusetts, 1971.

[2] Arrow, K. J., and F. H. Hahn, *General Competitive Analysis*, Holden-Day, San Francisco, 1971.

[3] Chamberlin, E. H., *The Theory of Monopolistic Competition*, Harvard University Press, Cambridge, Massachusetts, 1933.

[4] Cornwall, R. R., The Concept of General Equilibrium in a Market Economy with Imperfectly Competitive Producers, Working Paper Series No. 20, Department of Economics, University of California, Davis, October 1972 (cited with the kind permission of the author).

[5] Cournot, A., *Recherches sur les Principes Mathématiques de la Théorie des Richesses*, M. Riviere et Cie, Paris, 1838. English translation by N. T. Bacon, *Researches into the Mathematical Principles of the Theory of Wealth*, Macmillan, New York, 1897.

[6] Dorfman, R., P. A. Samuelson, and R. Solow, *Linear Programming and Economic Analysis*, McGraw-Hill, New York, 1958.

[7] Gabszewicz, J. J., and J. Vial, Oligopoly "à la Cournot" in a General Equilibrium Analysis, *Journal of Economic Theory*, 4, No. 3, June 1972.

[8] Gale, D., On Equilibrium for a Multi-sector Model of Income Propagation, *International Economic Review*, 5, No. 2, May 1964.

[9] Gale, D., and H. Nikaido, The Jacobian Matrix and Global Univalence of Mappings, *Mathematische*

Annalen, 159, 1965. Also included in P. Newman, ed., *Readings in Mathematical Economics,* Vol. I: *Value Theory,* The Johns Hopkins Press, Baltimore, Maryland, 1968.

[10] Hawkins, D., and H. A. Simon, Note: Some Conditions of Macroeconomic Stability, *Econometrica,* 17, 1949. Also included in P. Newman, ed., *Readings in Mathematical Economics,* Vol. I: *Value Theory,* The Johns Hopkins Press, Baltimore, Maryland, 1968.

[11] Karlin, S., *Mathematical Methods and Theory in Games, Programming and Economics,* Vol. I, Addison-Wesley, Reading, Massachusetts, 1959.

[12] Lange, O., *Price Flexibility and Employment,* Cowles Commision for Research in Economics, Monograph No. 8, Trinity University Press, San Antonio, Texas, 1944.

[13] Morishima, M., Some Properties of a Dynamic Leontief System with a Spectrum of Techniques, *Econometrica,* 27, No. 4, October 1959.

[14] Morishima, M., *Equilibrium, Stability and Growth,* Oxford at the Clarendon Press, 1964.

[15] Negishi, T., Monopolistic Competition and General Equilibrium, *Review of Economic Studies,* 28, 1961.

[16] Negishi, T., *General Equilibrium Theory and International Trade,* North-Holland, Amsterdam and London, 1972.

[17] Nikaido, H., Balanced Growth in Multi-sectoral Income Propagation under Autonomous Expenditure Schemes, *Review of Economic Studies,* 31, 1964.

[18] Nikaido, H., *Convex Structures and Economic Theory,* Academic Press, New York and London, 1968.

[19] Nikaido, H., *Introduction to Sets and Mappings in Modern Economics,* translated into English by K. Sato from the original Japanese edition (Iwanami Shoten, Tokyo, 1960), North-Holland, Amsterdam and London, 1970.

[20]   Robinson, J., *The Economics of Imperfect Competition*, Macmillan, London, 1933.

[21]   Stackelberg, H. von, *Marktform und Gleichgewicht*, Verlag von Julius Springer, Wien und Berlin, 1934.

[22]   Triffin, R., *Monopolistic Competition and General Equilibrium Theory*, Harvard University Press, Cambridge, Massachusetts, 1940.

Index

Library of Congress Cataloging in Publication Data

Nikaido, Hukukane, 1923–
     Monopolistic competition and effective demand.
     (Princeton studies in mathematical economics; 6)
     Bibliography: p.
     1. Prices—Mathematical models. 2. Income distri-
bution—Mathematical models. 3. Equilibrium (Economics)
I. Title. II. Series.
HB221.N54   339.2   74-25623
ISBN 0-691-04206-3

Milton Keynes UK
Ingram Content Group UK Ltd.
UKHW021952090624
443913UK00008B/301